Shepherd's Pie

Shepherd's Pie

by

Norbert F. Gaughan

THE THOMAS MORE PRESS
Chicago, Illinois

ISBN 0-88347-095-0

Special thanks to Pepperidge Farm, Inc. for permission to
print the recipe for Shepherd's Pie from *The Margaret
Rudkin Pepperidge Farm Cook Book*.

CONTENTS

FOREWORD

It may be that some will be disturbed that a bishop apparently speaks lightly of holy things, that there is levity and a preoccupation with the transitory books, fads, magazines. Why, they may say, does he not speak of holy matters, of spiritual values in a reverent way?

This author agrees with George Orwell, English essayist and novelist, that much too often orthodoxy is interpreted as meaning dull and flat. As Krister Stendahl says in *Paul Among Jews and Gentiles:* "It is my conviction that theology is too serious to allow humans to think theologically without playfulness and irony. To try to be as serious as the subject would be arrogant, and could lead the hearer/reader to believe that I considered everything to be precisely as I describe it. Of late I have become even more convinced of the theological necessity of irony—and of its nobler cousin humor—as a safeguard against idolatry. I believe that to be a reason why Jesus chose to speak in parables, most of which have a humorous twist. And the Jewish tradition, rabbinic, hasidic, and contemporary, is marked by a persistent cultivation of the telling of stories with a humorous slant—a point often missed by 'serious' theologians."

That concept has been helped along by Henry Fairlie, writer for *The New Republic,* in his book *The Seven Deadly Sins Today.* He cites an English writer, Monckton Milnes, in "Memoir of Thomas Hood." It is a text every churchman should make as his motto: "The sense of humor is the just balance of all the faculties of man, the best security against the pride of knowledge and the conceits of the imagination, the strongest inducement to submit with a wise and pious patience to the vicissitudes of human existence."

Such thoughts accurately reflect the mood of this book. An apology to those who do not agree, but it is this author's firm conviction. It is this spirit, that, God grant, permeates these musings.

The author expresses his thanks to all the writers of books, essays and articles who have provoked these thoughts. There are no extensive quotes, in the hope that you will want to go back and read an article or book on your own.

Special thanks are due to Miss Ursula Donaher who typed the script and proofread it, and to all the others whose patience has made it possible to think out loud. I am particularly grateful to many readers of other things that I have written over the years. It has been their encouragement that allows me to hope this book will find readers.

Much of this material appeared in another version in *The Catholic Accent,* Greensburg, Pa.

Part I

WORDS
AND THE WORD

There is little originality in the title of this book: "Shepherd's Pie." But the name is appropriate. There is something called "Shepherd's Pie."

In case anyone would like to whip up this satisfying dish, the following recipe may be of help. It comes from the *Margaret Rudkin Pepperidge Farm Cook Book:*

Preheat oven to 400°

    leftover lamb or beef
    salt and pepper
    mashed potatoes
    cooked carrots and peas
    two onions
    gravy or canned chicken broth

Put the meat through a chopper. Salt and pepper to taste. Place in a shallow baking dish. Add a layer of carrots and peas and onions thinly sliced. Add enough gravy or broth to moisten. Cover with mashed potatoes about ½ to 1 inch thick, dot with plenty of butter. Bake until potatoes are nicely browned (about ½ hour).

All recipes for "Shepherd's Pie" follow this basic format. Such recipes are plentiful; one can even be found in the "Scottish Women's Rural Institutes Cookery Book." This last may be too penitential for anyone, even as a suggested "Rice Bowl" meal for Lent.

The ingredients are always the same: beef or lamb, preferably left-over, seasonings, some gravy and mashed potatoes in a thin layer. Before anyone attempts to draw the conclusion that this has something to do with the office of bishop in the United States or England, we hasten to add no intent is here to institute a connection. Though, come to think of it, a very lovely allegory in the florid medieval style could be provided on the subject. "Notice that the Shepherd's Pie begins first with the lamb, those whose care the shepherd is charged with. There is a mystery here; no shepherd should eat this dish, else the shepherd is derelict in his duty in allowing someone, even himself, to steal the lamb. Shepherd's Pie requires ample seasoning. The words of the bishop, the chief shepherd, must always be well seasoned. He must be worth his salt. He can expect to be peppered by criticism. The bishop must be able to give a good account when he and his brother bishops will be mustered before the Lord. The mashed potatoes signify that he can expect to be crushed by his duties at times, but he must be prepared to protect others from the heat. And the gravy—'only enough gravy to moisten.' The shepherd must not have too much gravy." Enough of that.

"Shepherd's Pie" also appears frequently on the luncheon menu at the Duquesne Club, a posh and exclusive private club in Pittsburgh. Even the rich prefer simplicity when it is well done. Simplicity we have in this book; that it is well done must be your judgment.

"Shepherd's Pie" was also chosen as the name for the Parish Council newspaper of Good Shepherd Parish in Alexandria, Virginia. This journal, by the way, published recipes for altar bread baked at home. Here, alas, we cannot be of help.

The word "shepherd" itself is in trouble. Biblical criticism reminds us that the shepherd's position was mangy (to match some of the beasts he watched). When the Lord Jesus applied "shepherd" to Himself, He made a breath-taking connection. Shepherds were the lowest of the low, most untrustworthy and definitely outcasts. It was apt that Luke used shepherds as a symbol of the kind of sinners to whom good news of the birth of Jesus was proclaimed. In fact, all those who aspire to shepherd's role and office in the Church should remember that these add up to: sinners first, whatever else later.

Subsequent history of the word "shepherd" shows it continues to emit bad vibrations. Eric Partridge's *Dictionary of Slang* demonstrates that it has continuously been associated with pickpockets, crooks or shady characters. Even the lowly weed, "Shepherd's Purse" has been so called because like a thief it steals land from all other plants. Another explanation given is that the

11

tiny little seed is said to resemble a shepherd's purse. What did the shepherd keep in his purse? Shepherd's Pie? Probably not. Possibly whatever he stole.

PASTORAL

To be a shepherd, then, in the Church (the title is not restricted to bishops) is no claim to glory or power. Yet possibly to clarify any undue aura of such, Vatican II made a sweeping change and promoted "pastoral." That word too has an ancient connotation. Already, however, in our word-killing culture, "pastoral" has been overused, overworked; it is a victim of overkill. "Pastoral" no longer carries its pristine meanings. In the deluge of explanation about "pastoral" after Vatican II, the word has been mangled. It has been asked to take on so many meanings, it is literally meaningless. Consider: there are documents on the "pastoral" role of bishops, books on the "pastoral" ministry, and courses in "pastoral" theology. The word is no longer restricted to hierarchical or even priestly usage. Religious women are involved in "pastoral" ministry, they do "pastoral" work, they share "pastoral" concerns, which is certainly proper. Include then, laity too.

The word takes a primary Christian meaning from Christ the Good Shepherd, the "bonus pastor." Yet when one bishop said, in a kind of nonexplanation, that the pastoral office of a bishop is to be like Jesus the Good Shepherd, what did he really say? He presumed that "good" and "shepherd" as applied to Jesus have specific meaning and are accepted by all as explicitly definable, at least in practice. Archbishop Bernardin of Cincinnati tried to cut through the maze by pointing out that the word "pastoral" really means "practical," that is, that concern which should be exercised in a particular problem, for the spiritual welfare of those concerned, whether individuals or groups. But this brings it back to judgment, prudence. If so, "pastoral" always runs the risk of becoming "subjective" and debatable.

A historian of the medieval period, Walter Ullmann, points out in a number of places that "pastoral," both in its Hebrew original meaning and as expressed by Christ in His command to Peter, "Feed my sheep" (John 21:21), was a word which always carried legal connotations. It meant something like "to judge"—that is, to judge and decide a controversial issue so as to make the final decision. The pastoral office concerns the keys of Peter as much as the crosier of the shepherd. But such is our culture, few want to be judged, even in matters ecclesiastical. Our relaxed attitudes and our hatred of "legalism" have brought this about: few in authority want to "judge."

In the continuing attrition of language in our day, a person could equally defend any one of the following meanings for "pastoral." To be "pastoral" is:

1) To do good (whatever that means).
2) A pastoral person never hurts anybody. This sounds similar to Cardinal Newman's "a gentle-

man is one who never does harm to another."
"Pastoral" is one who never hurts.

3) What is "pastoral" can be decided by one versus another—even if there is some implied authority relationship. I can present my idea of what is good against what you think is good.

4) Sometimes "pastoral" is used to mean what is good for the greatest number. This was used often in the past, even if it meant removing an individual from a position and job. In the process he may be hurt but it's for the greater good. Thus, Caiphas could have been pastoral.

If "pastoral" includes the concept of shepherd as Jesus was, that means that to be pastoral . . .

5) Is to do what God wants done, as you see it; or . . .

6) As Jesus would have done; or . . .

7) What Jesus would want you to do here and now; or . . .

8) What *I think* Jesus would want you to do if He were here.

Again: subjective interpretations are involved, including the risk to be challenged. If one applies the word personally . . .

9) A pastoral work is one which will help me grow spiritually, interiorly. Yet does that mean to grow as *you think* I should grow, or . . .

10) To grow as *I want* to grow?

Once more: possibility of conflict exists. Does this mean . . .

11) That "pastoral" for me is to develop myself without regard for others?

We are in murky waters. Yet we have only scratched the surface. St. Paul's letters to Timothy are called "the Pastoral Epistles." They are said to be guidelines for Timothy, Titus and their helpers "to rule and sanctify their Christian converts" (to rule, i.e., to judge). St. Ignatius of Antioch told Polycarp that to be pastoral, Polycarp should defend his subjects against heretics. He had to be vigilant for their spiritual and temporal welfare. St. Cyprian thought that as pastor he had to instruct his clery in their daily conduct. St. Gregory of Nazianz defined "pastoral" as, "the art of arts and the science of sciences in that it concerned itself with the rule of men." St. Ambrose lived "pastorally" and he corrected even the Emperor. Gregory the Great wrote "rules for the pastoral life," which indicated that the prayer and holiness of the priest made him "pastoral." The Council of Trent was "pastoral" because it tried to create anew a zealous clergy against the clerics who had left their "pastoral duties" unattended. The great saints and writers of the Counter-Reformation were "pastoral." Today it is stylish to call them "reactionary" and "outmoded."

You see, "pastoral" is always to be understood in its culture and time. But for us these are still days of opposing views, debates on use and abuse of authority, and claims for self-development. If there is to be a discussion of what is "pastoral," be certain there is not much agreement on the meaning of the term. One man's pastoral activity may be viewed as bondage by another. One person's pastoral concern is held as restrictive and authoritarian by those who want "pastoral" to be "kind" at its best and sentimental do-goodism at its worst. It would be good if "pastoral" were given a rest. At least let's understand that it's not quite as simple as just being a "good shepherd." Who wants a shepherd, even a good one, these days? Yet, as has been said, "pastoral" and indeed all words, take their meaning from the cultural mood of the day. A "shepherd" in Christ's image must be concerned for things external and values unchanging. The shepherd must still set these values in the context of the cares and concerns of the time. For if being pastoral means knowing the ones for whom service is to be given, the shepherd and everyone who assumes that burden must know and judge all the things that affect the people.

Now we are faced with that most mysterious thing, "culture."

CULTURE

In this fast moving age, yesterday is ancient history, last month is primitive history, and last year is myth. Ideas, opinions, fashions have quick birth, short life and speedy demise. They flourish because our age of instant communication makes them quickly known and accepted without much critical analysis. Some theories are often championed as the latest solution to ills untold, staunchly defended as having lasting value, and upheld as the only one possible, the orthodox view. In short, while they are "in," they are "in."

Heaven help the benighted who would deny the value of the current orthodoxy. Who would want to swim against the tide of the latest "in" view? Who dares to gainsay that the latest proposal is not the harbinger of the Messianic age, because it does promise liberation from the outmoded past, salvation from the shackles of old fogey-ism?

A review of the last decades proves that quickly today's "in" becomes tomorrow's (or even tonight's) "out." It needs concentrated "in" watching to spot trends, to note developing patterns and to chart meteoric passage from "in" to "out." Does anybody remember the Death of God Theology? How many crash CCD programs have we undergone? The pace has accelerated. Even as one "theology" is on its way to becoming the "in" theology, its first death knell is already sounded by some who want to be "in" enough to declare it "out." Where are the pop heroes of yesterday's theology? The world of fashionable culture eats up its heroes quickly, to be as quickly thrown aside for the later fad. Which is sad. For each of the passing phenomena may have a value, if it is not overrated, overpraised, which does happen because of our penchant for the photographic and cultural hype. Some things are miniature; their qualities lie in their minuteness. They resist and will lose their good if they are magnified and blown-up. They should be valued for what they are. Not everything looks good through a macro-zoom lens.

So the shepherd, the pastor, must view these ephemeral things in a spirit of charity, even fondness, and with a certain smile. The pastor must believe that even in the passing events, the eternal perhaps does hide. On the other hand, it is also dangerous to label the transitory as eternal.

Yet there has been a view among some in the Church that the drama, motion pictures, books, magazines are demonic and dangerous. They rob us of our views of eternity. So we have scorned them. But people have not, they have been touched, shaped, molded.

So, the "in" and "out" *have affected* that supposedly timeless institution, the Church. We had acted as if it were impervious to cultural change, to changes of style in leadership, to "response" situations created by new demands or "perceived" needs (which never tell us who is the perceiver). Vatican II, among many other purposes, sought to raise such questions, and to provide, at least partially, some answers, or at least directions for answers. The Vatican Documents were reached by compromise (i.e., no one author, but amended, adapted, edited and re-edited). These lend themselves to ambiguities, to contradictory claims from holders of one view or another. It might appear that an ecclesiastical Supreme Court were needed to interpret specific meanings. There is: the Pope. But few of these matters reach him. Such questions are first handled at much lower levels: parochial, diocesan, regional, national. Here the first difficulty is often on the meaning of a word, a phrase, a paragraph.

MEANING PROBLEMS

Walker Percy (yes, the first name is Walker) is a Christian novelist. To put it another way, he is a Catholic, a scientist who has written four novels, *The Moviegoer, The Last Gentleman, Love in the Ruins, Lancelot.* He is a comic novelist, not in the sense of what passes for comedy today, the infantile parodies of Mel Brooks and others, the blackout TV skit comedy of Neil Simon. Percy is in the grand tradition of the comic, which frequently has a little tragedy nestling in its edges. None of his books have been made into movies yet because they defy that kind of simplification.

In 1975 Percy published a strange book, *The Message in the Bottle,* subtitled: "How Queer Man Is, How Queer Language Is, and What One Has To Do with the Other." It is a collection of essays or magazine pieces on the special place language has for man. Here Percy's writing is clear but "heavy." It is not everybody's specialty. Yet Percy does raise questions which may define areas of our present predicament in religion. He insists that the problem which faces the American Christian novelist is in part due to the fact "the vocabulary of Christendom is worn out." He continues: "The old words of grace are worn smooth as poker chips and a certain devaluation has occurred."

What does Percy mean? Without getting into philosophy or linguistics, can the issue be clarified? We know that words are only symbols. The human being grows up knowing the reality behind the symbols and learns to attach or identify the word symbols with the realities. For example, consider "water." The baby learns what water is before he can name it. When he uses the word as a human being there is the unstated supposition that everybody with whom he speaks will call upon the common knowledge of what water is. The child doesn't have to describe it, explain it. The word invokes the meaning. Of course it's a lot more complicated than that, but that's a place to start. Shades of meaning will change: sea water is different to the shore dweller than any water is to the man who lives in the desert. But both still know the meaning of water.

Apply this to the present problems in religious language and communications within the Church. One set of Catholics has grown up with a special vocabulary which meant to them certain realities: rosary, grace, holy water, Pope, sacraments, etc. These words were used. Those who employed them knew or presumed to know that the other was in touch with that same reality. But is that any longer true? Speak now to the generation educated post-Vatican II. The word "grace" means nothing. "Sanctifying grace" and "actual grace" carry even less import. They do not have such a background of understanding. The words we now use, instead of creating harmony, cause dissonance. We do not have the same reservoir of meanings on which to draw. Use words like "mortification," "self-denial." If you are, let's say, over 40, they have one meaning; to one under 30, another, if any, meaning. It's not anybody's fault. We must not blame or castigate. It's that in our rapid changes some words have dropped out of usage, others have acquired new meanings. It is in that sense that many religious books written before Vatican II have lost in part some of their ability to express to a new generation. The words used do not set up the same signals. Some words have been derided so that they have lost meaning: holy card, religious medal, holy water font. Other words have added bad meanings: authority, papal authority, institution, Holy Mother Church. Still others are emptied: matter and form of the sacrament, the seal and character of a sacrament, Limbo, indulgences, temporal punishment. The new generation of Catholics, however, has its own vocabulary. The use of the word "Bread" (just that, Bread) is a shock to the elder group. It hears reverberations of bread used to mean "money," or the cellulose that passes for bread today. Does "peace" have a different, deeper meaning to the young as contrasted with the old? The confusions of meaning go both ways.

When one speaks, he presumes the other is getting the same signals for the meaning as intended. When this does not happen immediately some persons are judged to be heretical, devoid of learning, irreligious, anti-Catholic. The others: old hat, out of touch, old fogeys. None of which are necessarily true. One generation is raised on a different set of meanings, with different answers or at least different questions. To restate it, the times and world views have changed fantastically and we constantly with them.

Is there no way out of this linguistic dilemma? Are we doomed to this double language? We hope not. But until we seek to create zones of understanding, zones of commonly accepted meanings, zones in which many varieties of persons are comfortable talking about understanding the Christian message, we may be trapped in this loss of communication.

Is there no common ground? Are there values that transcend time? Are there meanings we do hold in every age? What are the words (meanings) we will not give away, explain away or water down? What is the religious expectation of what a Catholic does hold or believe? What is it that makes it different to be a Catholic? Is it just something passed along in genes and chromosomes, in neighborhoods, or in upbringing? Or does it encompass a view of reality which we hold with others, without which we cannot live or make sense of life? That's what it should be.

SAINTS AS CONNECTIONS

Abigail McCarthy, separated wife of the presidential candidate Eugene McCarthy, was commenting on the difficulties in book promotion on TV shows. In *Commonweal* (August 5, 1977) she spoke of the value-setters, the opinion-makers (one suspects she meant mostly the TV talk show hosts and the people who appear with them), and declared they are in fact hostile to any kind of literary art. They publicly admitted they did not read novels. She deduced that they do not read anything else, except possibly the non-books which proliferate today. She quoted Henry Fairlie (writer for *The New Republic*) to the effect that "we in America have lost our common sources of allusion." That is to say, it is a rare American who can respond to the names of Huck Finn, Tom Sawyer, let alone Ahab, the captain from "Moby Dick," or even Nimrod, one of the characters mentioned in the early chapters of the Bible. That thought should be pursued.

Any teacher at a college level admits he can make no effective reference to a person or act which took place more than ten years earlier. Ask a student if he has read Shakespeare's "Julius Caesar" or has he ever seen it acted, and for any college class the answer is, no. Has the student, who heard of Napoleon, ever read Stephen Zweig's biography, or any other? In a recent class, references were made to the French Resistance, and nobody (and they were all under 25) knew what the French Resistance was, and against what it was resisting.

So this is a special situation. As was said, we of a middle-aged generation assume that there are certain principles, characters, common referents to which we can allude. We are wrong. It is not merely a matter of language, or word-change. (For example, to any modern young Catholic, "transubstantiation" is simply a meaningless word.) The problem goes deeper. We have no common heroes and heroines of the Faith to speak about together. With the decline of hagiography—that is, the lives of the saints—do any of our young people know much about the saints? In some parishes when administering Confirmation this author has been unable to find out from any of the young people just who the patron saint of the church was. But then you can ask, why should they? This may be correct, except each Sunday they are gathered together in a church under the name and patronage of that saint. Can we not presume they should know something about that? That presumption is false. It cannot be made. Soon even the modern saints, or the modern heroes, will be lost. We cannot speak of John XXIII. We cannot speak of Father Serra. We cannot speak of anybody except those who happen to be "in." Thus, it is possible to refer to Martin Luther King because some Catholic textbooks for CCD do speak of Martin Luther King and John Kennedy and Cesar Chavez as kinds of modern saints or would-be heroes. To wander further, is Church History still taught at all in parochial schools? Possibly not in CCD courses because time is so short there is no opportunity to give even a cursory glance at the treasures of Church History. But how about at least in a Catholic grade school? Odds are it is highly unlikely that this is a required course, or that if anything, it is ever entered into with any depth.

When we speak, therefore, of common referents, the student may know vaguely who St. Augustine is, or Thomas Aquinas, but will he have heard anything of the heroic deeds done early in the Church by saints? Will he know anything of St. John Chrysostom? Will he have heard anything about Thomas More? Will he have been told that he is one in bond with the missionary, Francis Xavier, and should learn of his indefatigable pouring out of himself for the Faith? Probably not. Hence we cannot speak from a presumed position that the saints are known and recognized by the young.

The calendar of saints has been somewhat reduced. Still, it was not an attempt to get rid of all the saints (except those of dubious or spurious claims to sanctity). But does a homilist explain St. Martin of Tours when his feast day comes around?

Will he speak about St. Augustine of Canterbury? Unlikely. So the question deserves to be asked. What is being done to fill up this vacuum?

How do we establish our roots in Catholicism? We are not speaking exclusively of matters of faith, which must be grounded in the Lord Jesus. But should we not "praise famous men," those brothers and sisters with whom we share that faith, who in different times and in different ways successfully lived that faith and provide "role models" for us. With change of time and place, the example of saints is just as meaningful for the young. Saints can inspire heroism and instill a desire to emulate virtues. Alas, such an attempt has been cast aside in order to inculcate attitudes or viewpoints of social value.

Abigail McCarthy was right. Not only is there hostility to art in literary form, there is also hostility today to older versions of sanctity. Such life examples are pushed aside as irrelevant and impossible for the modern age. This shows how ignorant we really are. Possibly when we talk "evangelization," the first thing to do is to lay down our anchors and fix our place in what we call the continuity of faith. If tradition means anything, it means that the faith which Jesus taught, which the Apostles preached, was lived in diverse ways by saints in the 3rd, 5th, 10th, 15th and 20th centuries. Yes, what we need badly to do is rediscover our roots, our referents. When we talk about what it means to be a Catholic, we will not be speaking from our own solipsistic time, but rather from a background of values we all know in some way which used to be called the Communion of the Saints.

Yet the varied interpretation of meanings persists. Beyond the meanings are sides, values attached to the meanings. This has led to a dichotomy, piously but wrongly invoked by those who wanted to establish values between "old Church" and "new Church." For depending on meaning to each, well-intentioned people could be assigned a place on either side of any position. Yet here again this is too easy, too simplistic. Such judgements are based on opinions being passed off as eternal truths.

OPINIONS

Editor Lewis Lapham of *Harper's* magazine had a good idea in the 1976 summer issue of the magazine. He spoke of "Received Ideas," and said: "The trouble with most conversations these days is that they depend almost entirely upon the exchange of received opinions. People do not have the time to think about what they are saying, and so they rely on an inventory of informed views that make sense in all sectors of enlightened discourse." Mr. Lapham observed how passing it all is; this year's opinions are next year's discards. Such opinions—note that, opinions, not truths or facts—change with the seasons. To illustrate, Lapham listed the summer of '76, "received opinion," i.e, Legitimate authority—no longer exists.

Nobody can command his own family, much less the state.

This leads us to suggest some "received opinions" in religious, i.e., Church news. But as has been said, polarization has cut us asunder. Thus any given opinion could probably be challenged by an opposite view, or a place between both.

Vatican II—The best thing that hit the Church. The worst thing to hit the Church. It is irrelevant.

Charismatics—The only thing that will save religion. Try it, you'll like it. It's not for me.

Ordination of Women—God will never allow it. The Church needs it to survive. If God wanted it, He'd have made His Son a daughter.

Sisters—The sooner they get back into their habits, the sooner will Catholic schools be saved. Habits are unimportant. Way ahead of the priests and bishops. A dying class.

Contraception—A dead issue. Why bring that up? If the Church gives in here, it will collapse. More important things than that need defending. It is the source of all our troubles today.

Sacrament of Reconciliation—What's that? Simply means: general absolution. Longer but less confession. Yawn.

Cardinals—Glad we got some in America, but what are they doing about whatever the local problem is? Authoritarian. Out of touch.

The Liturgy—Same old thing every Sunday. The only thing to save the church. Drives people away. Not where the action is.

Priests—Why don't they settle down and do their work like we do? Dedicated. Irrelevant. Better than ever.

CCD—It was much better back when it was plain old catechism. Has made young more aware of social needs of Gospel.

Money—The new Church talks a lot about love but it still asks for money. Too much in the Church. The Church should give it all back to the poor.

Deacon—Is that a seminaran? What does he do? We had one for a while. Why is he married?

Abortion—It's terrible, but still, if my daughter were involved I don't know what I'd do. The only issue. Why they hate us Catholics.

Parish Council—Who elected those guys? Father never uses them. They have too much say.

Sermons—Not where the real world is. Too long. All talk. No instruction in religion.

Pope—Doesn't he know the Church must become democratic? This is America. What does he know about it? Overburdened. I feel sorry for him.

Bishops—Nice guys, but too easy on the troublemakers in the Church. Should retire sooner. Why don't they do something about the situation?

The Family—Not like when I was a kid. Doesn't have enough say. Breaking up.

Prayer—Nobody does it except in church. Why do they have trouble praying? Nobody ever had to teach me.

Mysticism—Buddhas, incense and colored lights. Everybody has it. Hare Krishna people.

Catholic Colleges—Place where kids lose their faith. Not needed. Only place to send your children in today's secular world.

Bishops' Meetings—What comes out of it? Need more of them. Too secret. Isn't that like a convention?

Catholic Schools—Should be kept open at any cost (except to me). Cannot be saved. Need more of them. Too much money spent on keeping them open.

The Church—Has no right to tell me what to do. Irrelevant in modern society. Needs restructuring.

Hymns—They all drag so. When will they write them like the old ones? Too Protestant. I can't sing them.

The Devil—I don't believe in him, but did you see the movie? People are more afraid of him than of God.

You get the idea? Always there are the current unexamined "received opinions." Let one Catholic bring up a subject and some good Catholic will say something like the above almost immediately or challenge said statement by enunciating its contrary, or contradictory.

Not enough creative thinking is being done or will be done. Mostly folks will rehash, repeat, regurgitate. Little is ever added to the store of information about the subject or lack of it. So this passes for discussion in most of the conversations about religious subjects by the populace, and include us in.

In such discussions each side also believes it is right, and it is wrong for the other to question anybody's sincerity. In fact, to do so is considered most unchristian, even if, in fact, you are convinced that the person was not being truthful. It was not that he lacked sincerity; you should just presume the person has persuaded himself of the matter.

SINCERE

When Conrad Birdie, the Elvis-like pop singer of the Broadway musical "Bye Bye Birdie" sang, "You've got to be sin-cere," he well demonstrated the modern schizophrenia about sincerity. The character in the play, Birdie, was the creation of a press agent, a phony, a slicked-up, hypoed caricature of youth. But wherever he appeared he was greeted enthusiastically, mobbed, and idolized by a youthful corps which thought he was real, that he was truly "sincere."

The quest for sincerity in our times has become one of many kinds of search among men for an eminent personal quality. Lionel Trilling has produced a long and involved examination of this illusion: sincerity as the only value. David Martin, professor of sociology at London's School of Economics, also dissected it in "The Naked Self" (*Encounter*, June 1973). He thought the search for sincerity was really an attempt to flee demands in life for the rules, roles and relationships society demands.

Martin called this philosophy the "heresy of choice." It says that the "logic of the spontaneous self" demands man's every action must be free, spontaneous, and not to be made on the basis of his "role" in society, his function, or because of rules imposed from above—that is, from authority external to self. In current parlance, only the immediate self is genuine, and even basic. All structures are not genuine, not even natural. They are self-limiting, thus insincere and not genuine.

What really is at the heart of the matter is another concept: the search for order. "Order" is thought of as a set of relations, perceived by most men, in which duties proper to a man, established by his place in the order, are incumbent upon him. These duties involve rules, which are at the base of all social regulation, which help us grasp easily our "role," our place, to become "familiar" with it. Order and rule imply purpose (another bad word), which sees some rational explanation for human activity, and even talks about an order established by powers or forces outside human history (God). That's why those institutions whose essence involve order: family, the school, and church, are downgraded by the proponents of sincerity and genuineness.

There is little doubt that the disorder of modern life and harassment by social pressures have attacked the family, which it is said can no longer teach order. It must superimpose order and that's bad. Hence the reported demands of some young people to "be themselves," the accusations that parents are usually "phony," and certain demands for "participatory democracy," which in effect is to make all equal in authority in the family structure. This leads to chaos.

There appear new educational theories which place a premium on sincerity in the search for what Martin calls "The Naked Self." These bring disorder in a place where the young are supposed to learn order, their "place" in the universe, and their relations (governed by rules) with others. The need for "grading" in school is challenged today—since all that counts is to be true and genuine. Yet "grading" helps to establish order, to promote growth, to challenge development—i.e., to bring order into the unordered chaotic life of youth.

One place where the mad rush for sincerity has created disorder is the Church. Of course, in the eye of God (and also the Church) every human is equally worthy and valuable. But the Church has God's word too, and the tradition of its believers. It asks that believers grow and learn, that they assume a place in the Church, that they accept a Church in which "roles" are important.

Instead, the Church has been barraged by demands for relevance, for meaningful relationships, and the acceptance only of what "I can find personally meaningful." We are asked to reject for ourselves (and implicitly for others) all those things, old and new, that we find not meaningful. Naturally, priests, teachers and leaders who are "sincere" are esteemed. Any who ask to hold to the "faith of the Fathers," to the teaching of tradition, to the rules from Rome, are automatically labelled as phony, insincere and ungenuine. This, even though Christianity is an historical faith, to bring out, as Christ said, "things new and old," and to establish God's order in the present, which it has learned from its past.

Sincerity should demand in all three—family, school, Church—responsibility. Responsibility implies that a person sees and accepts rules and obligations and is held accountable for them. "To people, yes," say the searchers for sincerity, "but to institutions, no!" Yet, what are institutions but groupings of others, who with you, accept responsibility and hence accountability for behavior according to rules and patterns.

In the end, to be genuine and sincere is to be more than merely spontaneous. It is to grasp a picture, a pattern of self, partly formed from roots of others, molded and shaped by and in relationship to others, to bring the order of a pattern of self into the disorganized chaos of birth. As Martin says, it is "to be present at a miraculous birth," the birth of the true self, not the naked, untrammeled self. It must be the self of one who accepts a place, always modifying it, but a place to share in the making of the order which helps men to discover themselves.

Meaningful, relevant—who determines what these are? Individuals? Causes? Ideologies? The mood is here to make converts, to "brainwash," or simply the desire of some to "educate" the others into opinions. Party A decides he is right and all others are just not as informed, up-to-date, scholarly, or versed in the fields in which Party A is expert. Hence the need of Party A to raise the consciousness of the others, the not-so-well versed (as it is claimed). Simply: what do these know-betters do?

KNOW-BETTERS

Those were the good old days, weren't they, when all you had to worry about was theology; no psychology, sociology, nor anthropology. Today to be able to approach any group of professionals in religious causes, you don't really need to know any of the above. But it helps if you're able to inject "in" words or concepts from those fields.

Yet, it would be better, if to know some of the problems that face religion today, you would be conversant with some of the central ideas discussed by practitioners of the above. Peter L.

Berger, the readable professor of sociology, is also a Protestant theologian. He always joins his two disciplines in interesting ways. In *Pyramids of Sacrifice: Political Ethics and Social Change* (1976), he attacked some of the ideologies being passed around disguised as religion. As he did in the magazine *Worldview* in 1975, Berger was particularly hard on that technique of brainwashing called "consciousness raising." It is timely because consciousness raising of a kind is being done by Catholic teachers and educators as if it were a Gospel mandate. Berger more correctly sees such a practice as unchristian and immoral.

"Consciousness raising" began as a technique to train Brazilian natives how to read and write. But this was only the secondary purpose. The materials handed them to read, discuss, and to write about were political, to change their understanding of their present situation, and to prepare for a revolution (violent or not, but certainly political). This technique was then two-pronged. It pretended to help people only to read and write, but it was intended to educate them politically to change the government. Now consciousness raising has been adopted by religious opinion-makers in America as a tool to promote their views of what religious bodies and persons should be doing. All those organizations which seek to bring the consciousness of people to accept what this organization says they must think, are followers of the system.

Berger correctly asked important questions. Whose consciousness is being raised? Always the other guys', the poor, "the religiously illiterate," the religiously uneducated, those who do not know what's good for them, for the religion, for the Church. Berger's other question: who does the raising? The answer: we, the elite, the vanguard, the intellectuals, the upper class, better educated, more concerned. In this viewpoint the act is not only unjust, but immoral. "We" who raise the consciousness accept as a fact that we are right and they are wrong. In this proud and arrogant assumption, we assume that we will help THEM to become as concerned, or caring, or religious, or social gospel-oriented as we are. Berger is right when he calls this more properly, "conversion." It is a mixed bag which says I know the truth better than you do, and I want to help you to become as understanding as I am. Yet to do so is to set the priorities for others. When we think we know what's important for everybody else, that's dangerous. You see, no one is more conscious than anyone else. We are conscious of different things. Each of us lives in his own world in a way, in which we are conscious of what is important for us.

This may explain some resentment among laypeople arising from the occasional patronizing attitudes of a few clergy and religious. Some laymen say: "Who said that choosing the wines and lettuce cause is a high priority for my religious life? Who determined that any social action must be done as a protest if I am to be a 'real' Christian?"

This helps to explain other resistances. Some people still object to lay Eucharistic ministers. The "experts" say this practice is good for you; it will move the Mass faster. Some laymen have another consciousness, of the Eucharist as something special and reserved for ordained ministers. (We are not choosing sides.) The point is, one "consciousness" is different from another. There should be no lectures to the objectors that they are backward or resisting the Church, or whatever.

It is all very difficult. There are those who must teach officially. But if they do, they must instruct on all points where there are choices. There must be no presumption: "I am a priest; I am a nun; I am a CCD teacher. I know what is better for these people than they do," in matters of choice or taste or option.

This is a murky area. Yet if there are, as reported,swells of resentment within the Church, it is because one group wants to raise the level of "consciousness" of the other. It is not always that clear that the level chosen is one which is Church doctrine, or merely a priority or a preference or a choice made by the raiser. It may be a social program, a political objective, not necessarily religious. If anything, in such matters, teachers must be most careful and must not postulate that "those others" are ignorant and simple people, or don't know what's good for them, or are not with the Church, or are against Vatican II, and all that other nonsense. Maybe it would be better if the consciousness raiser would just simply say, "This is what I like and I don't care what you like."

But here again the problem of "meaning" surfaces. To sell these causes, each of these disciplines quickly adopts a vocabulary all its own. Still more confusion arises, for these manufactured words which have a more or less (mostly less) specific meaning are used in all the writing, discussion and proselytizing. They are known only to the practitioners of the trade. In short, they use "jargon."

JARGON

Every professional communicator in the Church, and by this we mean priests, teachers, deacons, CCD personnel, should read Edwin Newman's books on the abuse of the English language. He blames TV mostly for the decline. He makes a strong plea as one versed in the art of communication and meanings of words.

Religious communicators should pay heed, for they slip much too easily into the jargon of the day. Quickly they adapt to modish words, borrow neologisms (badly made-up new words), and willingly risk violating language, this great gift of God, in such a way as to conceal truth. A few examples could illustrate the point.

The prestigious Canon Law Society of America one day proudly announced that it possessed a "think tank." First and most obvious, it was not called a "thought tank." The verb "think" was used as an adjective. Possibly in a "think tank" there is no thought, only would-be thinkers. But why "tank?" The word itself conjured bad images. A tank is a container; but creative thought must be uncontained. The slangy use of the word "tank" left this new device open to all kinds of misinterpretations. Too often the pronouncements of "thinkers" just out of a "think tank" would convince that the thinkers were more "tanked" than thoughtful. How many thinkers can a "think tank" contain? Given the tendency of most American males, especially clerics, to run overweight (most clerical medical exams begin: middle-aged, slightly obese man), are there less thinkers in a "think tank" if too many of them are overweight? In that tank, which is also the place into which policemen place drunken offenders overnight (hence the word "tanked"), does the tank contain them—i.e., restrict them, or does the tank expand with the amount of "think" produced? You see?

Sad to say, each discipline creates its own jargon. Catholic educators who frequently talk with their peers in secular education, talk the same jargon. (Should not some Catholic educator write an article, "How I Went from Input to Interface in Two Short Years"?) One borrowed word is "enrichment." There are many "enrichment programs" in Catholic schools and CCD classes. But what is an "enrichment program?" Many years ago we learned that "enriched" was not necessarily good, when "enriched" flour first had the wholesomeness taken out, only to be added later. We paid more for "enriched" flour, which we might have had originally, without much fuss. Does "enrichment program" in CCD and Catholic education lingo mean a program which all should have had from the beginning? Does "enrichment" mean that not everybody's getting it? Why not? Does it mean that some will be less "rich" in the matter or content received from teachers? "Enrichment" hints possibly that there might be inequalities: those who are lucky or have personnel available will be enriched, while others will be left "poor" or at least less rich.

We have already mentioned minister-sociologist Peter Berger on the subject of "consciousness raising" in social issues. As was said, this implies the "raisers" know better than the "raised." It creates an impression of elitism and moral superiority. Berger asked, how can you raise "consciousness?" We are conscious, or not. Awareness may be better, but then who decides the things of which we must be "aware?"

Jargon is a major problem in the *Catechetical Directory*. Consider a text in one of the original drafts. Who can understand, without help, this: "The foundations of self-acceptance, trust and autonomy will be both reinforced and modified. The child's unquestioned acceptance of self is not translated into awareness of specific personal talents or their absence. Unqualified trust of others is also adapted through experiences to exclude certain persons or situations. The child's expression of autonomy is adjusted by the experience of the autonomy of others." Would parents understand all this?

"Speaking plainly"—that's the issue. To speak plain is to speak honest (true?). Technical jargon becomes an occult language only to the initiated. Modish language brags that we are up on the latest. In matters of faith there should be neither fashions nor modes. What is asked of all of us within the Church, priest, teacher, parent, youth, according to St. Paul, is to be able to make a reasonable account of the faith which we hold. A reasonable account would imply language which is open to reason, not needing to be deciphered nor decoded. It is never to be language only for an elite. But it has always been thus. Language matches people, and we have different kinds of languages, and always have had.

CANT VERSUS JARGON

In our age when words are cheap and plentiful, at a time when communication is our greatest need, its means most abundant, and its results most meagre, it could be advantageous to reflect upon "private" languages, or the ways in which words become so special that they cease to convey meaning.

"Cant" is probably the oldest word to indicate this kind of language. Coming from a French word, "singing," cant began as a reference to the whining, singing tone used by beggars. In time it

referred to expressions used, and generally understood only by members of a particular sect or occupation. It also developed with it a meaning of
contempt, and particularly the insincere use of
religious or pious phraseology.

"Argot" was a different kind of word. Argot
was used to describe the kind of secret, esoteric
language used by the group, or occupation. It was
intended to be secret, and to hide its meanings
from the uninitiated. It began as the tool of thieves,
using extravagant words and strange terms to conceal its true meaning from outsiders, to hide secret
meanings.

"Slang," often used as synonymous with cant or
jargon, has come to mean the popular but not approved vogue of words that quickly come and go
(some stay). No one quite knows where the word
"slang" got its beginnings. Was it the special cant
of illiterate or disreputable persons? Notice how
we still use phrases as: "He can sling the language!" Does it come from the Norwegian word
for "sling the jaw," i.e., twist it, abuse it, by such
words? Who knows except that there is nothing
that ages so quickly as slang. These words mostly
have a brief and hectic life.

Then there is "jargon," of which we have
spoken. The basic meaning of the word jargon is to
emit confused or unintelligible sounds. Noisiness is
a part of jargon. Jargon began in the Old French
word for throat or gullet. Jargon came to mean any
noise made in the throat, such as the warbling of
birds. Some poets referred to the "jargonning of

birds." But in time, jargon accepted a meaning of a special language, a special vocabulary of some branch of study or science. Such specialized talk is, of course, unintelligible to laymen. So jargon became a term of contempt, but today simply means "trade talk," the easy words that come to be used by practitioners of a technology or trade. There is "space jargon," "computer jargon," etc.

All very well, but the problem arises when words, which began their life used only by the "initiated," are used not only by the initiated but also by the uninitiated, loosely and indiscriminately. Such words become non-communicative. By being used out of their context, they are either unintelligible, or convey no meaning. In fact, they often become easy crutches for people who do not want precise meaning, nor to be pinned down. This is much of the fun of comedian Norm Crosby. His "fractured English" is a keen insight to the ways "special words" mean nothing when used merely for sound.

In this age of "verbal overkill," a multiplication of words does not imply a multiplication of meaning. Quite the contrary is true. It is one of the great riches of language that we can borrow words from other tongues, or from other classes—this is good. But at a time when human relations and our "interpersonal" gropings are so important, it is tragic that we fall so often into cant, argot, jargon or slang. What is worse is that such words have become so trite, so stale, that they have, in effect, resulted in this, that neither the user, nor the hearer actually hear the words. They become merely throat sounds—i.e., jargon.

This is particularly true of discussions where words are used about faith, religion, God, in non-reflective ways. A newer branch of theology these days is concerned about "God language," words which no longer convey the realities about God that they perhaps once did in other cultures, or other times. Today such phrases are being questioned because they do, in fact, say nothing to too many people.

It was Louis Evely who said that when you come to somebody with your problem, and having heard you, he responds, "I'll pray for you," what his words actually mean is that "There's nothing I can (or will) do for you." There are too many sermons which use glibly choice phrases such as "the will of God," "goodness," "holiness," which are in fact clerical "trade talk" and too often do not mean enough, if anything, to the layman. These phrases, culled from old sermon books and theological tracts, come easily to tongues trained in theological talk, but mean little or nothing to the hearers. What are the poor people to do when the sermonizer talks about "eschatological," "existential," "the ground of our being," and the like?

The greatest victim of such cant and jargon is "love"—that word thrown around so indiscriminately as the easy solution to all problems. Whose love? Whose definition? What are some of the hidden, deeper implications of the "love" about which you speak so easily? For example, no matter how you rhapsodize, Christian love is not synonymous with "love" as used in other cultures, other settings. But who bothers to explain, to be precise? Easier to mouth the words, let them come jargonning out of the throat. That way neither speaker nor hearer has to think. Or to put it another way: in questions of faith, and human understanding, and especially in love, one must be more than usually careful to be precise, clear and intelligible.

Your talk may be another man's jargon—or cant—but it will probably not be his or your way to understanding.

But language pains creep into even the highest levels of teaching, even among the bishops of the United States, and particularly through their "civil service," the bureaucrats who prepare statements to be issued by the Conference of Bishops.

LANGUAGE PAINS

At just one meeting of ordinary clergymen (priests/ministers), the following words were used interminably as part of a discourse on pastoral relations (relation of clergymen to parishioners): "intercommunication" (is there an "extra-communication?"), "interface" (does that mean you put one face sandwiched between two others?), "outreach" (can you reach into yourself?), "over-breadth" (we wonder what underbreadth is like), and "disvalue," which may or may not be done in a "continuum." All this is bad enough, but when such officialese creeps into official teaching documents and publications of bishops (singly and collectively), it jars. A document on Catholic/ Jewish relations from the National Office of the Conference of Bishops stated that the Jewish people have always desired a "peoplehood." What is a peoplehood? Could it not just have been said that the Jews conceive of themselves as a "people?" Pursue just this one word, "peoplehood." Note what happens in the slow agglomerations which are used in attempts to clarify but instead obscure.

If you would start with a "peoplehood," then the quality of those wanting a peoplehood is that they would demonstrate "peoplehoodness." If such people are able to achieve this quality they then could be said to possess "peoplehoodnessability." However, in order to do this, they must demonstrate that they have the capability or that this is possible. So, they must have "peoplehoodnessoperability." However, if they do not have this quality, it is moot as to whether they possess "peoplehoodnessnonoperability," or are just against it, victims of "antipeoplehoodnessnonoperability." Unless, of course, they are just members of that group, the possessors of "nonpeoplehoodnessoperability." Yet again, if they are against that concept, they hold "nonantipeoplehoodnessnonoperability." And so on.

Suffering suffixes! Sir Arthur Quiller-Couch, an English writer of past centuries, is the one who gave us the label of "jargon." Someone looking for a project to wed computer and language research could attempt to discover whether English (American) words generally have grown an inch or so in the last century.

This is not said to be clever; there may be deeper implications here. The philosopher, Ludwig Wittgenstein, a Viennese who achieved glory in England, claimed that to make one statement, an assertion, was to accept in faith the whole construct of language. Can we deduce that from the growing confusion of redundancy, paralyzing prefixes, insufferable suffixes, and sheer lack of intelligibility, that we are in a crisis of faith, a faith in our ability to communicate, to give simple information one to another? Faith in what, you ask? Faith in the other. Faith that we humans can or want to understand. Faith in ourselves as disseminators of truth and information. Do we really believe that what we want to say is valueless unless cloaked in the garments of stilted language? Have we lost faith in our common humanity, in the truths presupposed by language, that we are one family of man, made by the one God and Father? Or is it even loss of faith in God, a conviction that He has not given men the ability to comprehend, unless we rework language, unless the matter is chewed over, regurgitated, spewed forth and slopped around until not a single glimmer of meaning peeks through, but much confusion. Or is it that we just do not want to be pinned down? As one teacher put it, do we use language to hide the truth?

To restate it in another way, have we arrived at 20th century babble because we are trying to build a towering Babel of words, adverbs, adjectives, prefixes, suffixes, to use 25 words to achieve what one simple, honest word could do? All this is entirely possible.

Meanwhile, as each Sunday we are in the name of God to hear the bland pabulum that the Sacred Word has often been reduced to through the commonplace translations of the Bible into Americanese, we wonder: ah, religion, what crimes have been committed in thy name! We live today on the simple and wrong assumption that the ordinary Catholic is a simple-minded soul. Everything must either be reduced to the lowest, uncommon denominator, or it must be placed in the officialese, superinflated so much so that it becomes an exercise akin to making a souffle: the result—sweet, not palatable, and full of air.

Thank God for one thing, at least. It all seems to be slowing down. Or does it? "Conservatives" believe that everybody is tired, the new fields have been mined out, disappointment or dismay have set in, and it's only a matter of time till things are quiet enough for the "old" values to be reintroduced.

Contrary, "liberals" have decided to husband (male chauvinist word?) their energies and to concentrate on a few key issues. They did not always feel that way. But it may now be necessary—a regrouping of the forces.

NORBERT GAUGHAN

THE THEOLOGY OF THEOLOGY

When Father Raymond Brown, one of the greatest
Bible scholars of this century (not Bar-Jonah, bar
none), spoke in 1973 to the National Catholic Education Association, he noted one danger threatening renewal efforts in the Church as coming
from "ultra-liberals who scorn serious theology."
(He also cited another danger from ultra-con-
servatives, "who see in every investigation a
threat to the Faith.") The key word in the first
charge is "serious theology." There seems to be, in
these days of so many shortages, a serious short-
age of *that*. Concerning a book on theology published in 1973, one critic wrote: "The author
shows he has read widely on both sides of the
question, that he has given much thought to both
sides, and that hard planning has gone into the ex-
position of thought." He never told us if the result
was worth it.

If the Christian Church seems fragmented and
splintered, pity poor theology. It's in the same sad
condition. Once the queen of the ecclesiastical
sciences, theology has become the scapegoat for
our problems, with fingers of scorn pointed at it by
dubious bishops, uncompromising Catholics, or ra-
tionalizing Christians.

Still, theology may deserve some of the brickbats
thrown at it. Too often it uses Madison Avenue
techniques to promote itself (usually for bucks). An
unhappy result has been a naming game used to
sell the hottest and newest phase of theological
opinion. (Note: not study, not thought, but *opinion!*)

Once it was only theology: the science of the study of God. (More correctly, it was the science of man's study of God.) Next it was subdivided: dogmatic theology (study of doctrine), and moral theology (study of human actions based on God's [moral] law). But the name explosion of recent years has brought many "new" kinds of theology for our edification. In too short a time we have run the gamut (what is a gamut, by the way?).

First we had "Theology of the Secular City." Where is it now, alas?

We were given "Theology of Hope" (a valid study, since hope is a theological virtue), but despite continued good work by the Protestant theologian Jürgen Moltmann, that phase is scarcely mentioned anymore.

Scripture studies gave birth to "Incarnational Theology," but at least this was about God's dealings with men in the person of Jesus Christ.

The hottest item in latter years has been "Liberation Theology," which was translated by some eager souls into "Theology of Revolution." Despite some few positive ideas, that became more an ideology than a theology.

Michael Novak, who dabbles in what could be called "Ethnic Theology," proposed a "Theology of Evil" to help us through the Watergate trauma. We had also lived through Sam Keen's and Harvey Cox's "Theology of Wonder," which never really got off the ground. That was itself a reaction to the "God is Dead Theology." This was over-touted by the media for shock value and quickly went into the cemetery of pop theologies.

In later years we have had "Theology of Death," and the Holy Year, a few years ago, promoted "Theology of Reconciliation."

Meanwhile bishops, anxious to overcome some pop theological challenges, have counterattacked with others. Cardinal Manning of Los Angeles has proposed a "Theology of Commitment" to get us through the crisis in Christian marriage.

Not to be outdone, Protestant theologians suggested still others, as did Arthur Vogel, who branched out from "anthropological theology" (a hot item three or four years ago) to come up with "Body Theology."

As far as is known here, no one has come up with a specific "Charismatic Theology," or "Pentecostal Theology," although books are currently describing the phenomenon.

The point of these musings:

1) God is still the proper object of theology. But since it is man who theologizes (God does not), man, his nature and what concerns him in his relation to God, is always involved at the center.

2) This naming game is but an attempt to emphasize one aspect of a problem. It has value, except if, in an outburst of enthusiasm, it goes too far and overemphasizes the one facet to the detriment of the total view.

3) "Pop Theology" is no help. It besmirches the good name of theology (now held in disrepute by too many) by giving the impression that all theology is ephemeral, transient, or has no staying power.

4) What seems to be lacking was stated in the

opening paragraphs above. Father Brown decried the loss of serious theology. Too many jumpers-into-the-breach hurriedly develop emphases-types of opinions without proper thought, and lacking consideration of both (or as many as there are) sides of a question.

5) The most serious damage is a relic of the Nixon-Kissinger syndrome. Everything this Dynamic Duo did in the field of foreign diplomacy was "the best," "the greatest," "the most," "the wisest," etc. Is there no one, especially in theological studies, who will propose his thought in a modest way, not as the one, all-encompassing key or solution, but as a minor contribution to the further understanding of the mysteries involved in God and Man?

In short, less publicity, less promotion, and more hard work. Back to the drawing boards, men/women. Or as the typewriter exercise says, "Now is the time for all good men (and women) to come to the aid of theology."

Yet, it is true, things have apparently changed. It may be not just a change in religion, or theology. It may be that the fashion in intellectual practice has changed, and this affects the other two.

FADS AND FASHIONS

Theological fashion changes have slowed down for a while. There was a time when there was one every six months. It was supposed to be the latest, the best, the newest solution to all our woes. The theological fad (not named as such) was discussed in papers and magazines. A new book got things rolling. "In" priests preached about it frequently; seminarians debated it; everybody quoted choice phrases from it. Within six months that fad gave way to another, the newer. A new book by Karl Rahner comes out and it's barely noticed. Hans Küng tries to get discussions going with controversial articles, but nobody jumps into the fray. Catholic periodicals and controversial newspapers fill up space each week with repetition of last month's articles. What does the present situation signify?

Jean-Francois Revel, who wrote the book, *Without Marx or Jesus* (which never really took off in America), was in California talking at the Center for the Study of Democratic Institutions some time ago about "Intellectual Fashions." He saw these as a phenomenon of our times and noted their basic characteristics. They are as follows:

The first is that such an intellectual fad satisfied a need for "globalism," which is a complete and comprehensive explanation of reality. In days when there are so many complex and difficult disciplines, people want to find one theory, easily apprehended, by which one can explain all other complexities.

The second characteristic is that the success of the intellectual fashion has nothing to do with whether it is proven true or discovered to be wrong. It comes at the right moment, captures the fancy, everybody talks about it, it appears to be well grounded, and usually succeeds because it satisfies some emotional needs, or even societal cravings.

Next, these fashions must give birth to new words. They develop their own language. They allow the "in" people to exchange these words with knowing smiles and with the air of experts. Revel claimed that this vocabulary disappears after a while, depending on the length of the fashions—forty years, or four months, or even four hours. The old words are pushed out by new. There has to be an ever new "in" vocabulary.

Another aspect of these fashions is that they call upon some appearances of science to defend them. They take scientific words and ideas out of the relevant scientific field. In the process, these words lose their original meaning and become empty of their scientific meaning. (Notice how the word "relationship" is everywhere these days. It replaces "love," "friendship," and so on.)

The fifth characteristic, sadly true, develops when the majority of people attracted to the fashion never read the books from which it comes. People gain superficial knowledge of a few facts. They may make a general attempt to seize the skeleton of the idea, most gleaned from articles about the author of the fashion or his theories. Few plumb deeply into the sources.

Finally, these fashions pretend to explain more than they can. They seek to give the latest and most developed *opinon*. Their assertions are not always based on the realities.

Call it all "faddism"; but it is not new. It occurred in 4th century B.C. Greece, was present at the time of Christ, and appeared in 4th century A.D. Rome. When St. Paul visited Athens he noted, "I know you people always want to hear something new. Well, I have something new to tell you." He used their craving for fashion to his advantage.

This may explain the great wave of theological fashions we have had, one tumbling after another in the Vatican II period. As Peter Green says, "Controversies emerge not only when people have new ideas, but also when they suddenly wake up to realize that they no longer have the old ones." This does not explain why every so often, as now, there seems to be a drying up of theological ideas. It may well be that because for a time the intellectual fashions came and went so quickly, people have now moved on to other kinds of intellectual fashions. There occur the latest psychiatric solutions: "I'm Okay, You're Okay," or Transactional Analysis. There may be the latest diet fad, how to lose weight by eating, drinking, by not eating and drinking, and the like. In rearing children, Piaget is in, Bruno Bettelheim's on the way out.

No wonder that theological fashions are stilled at times. Yet we can always expect some resurgence. Possibly now someone is dreaming up a new way to explain modern man's relationship to God on the basis of the latest intellectual fashion. Who knows? There could be a book in the making, "God and Your Diet." There may even be one on "We're Okay, God's Okay." We're surprised that someone hasn't followed up Michael Novak and Father Greeley with a book on "Ethnic Theology," or with the seagull, "The Theology of Flying." But any respite, while it's going on, is very peaceful and enjoyable. It gives time for things to settle down.

One good thing evolves from this pressure to change everything all at once. In fact it may have even caused the decline. This is the failure of the meeting (theology by consensus, or democratic theology) to resolve major issues; in fact, they only get more complicated. The Call for Action Conference of 1976 may have been the first and last of such giant meetings. Even as Catholics debate the resolutions, and NCCB subcommittees discuss proposals, meetings as resolutions of problems possibly have reached their highpoint.

MEETINGS

Some time ago at a gathering of Church leaders in England, the late Cardinal Heenan, who rarely chose the popular way or the acceptable subject, told Protestant and Catholic leaders that the Christian Church is doing too much talking and discussing. As he put it, "Much of our pastoral effort is being stifled by the growing number of meetings, discussions and conferences to which bishops and priests are subjected." That remark was discounted immediately by not a few who said, "Look who's talking! It was bishops and cardinals that got us on this merry-go-round of meetings. Their Vatican II marathon discussion started it all."

Others will jump on Heenan's added words, "I think it likely that many who have left the priesthood, or the religious life, would still be with us if they had not dissipated their zeal in endless talking." That solution does seem a bit simplistic. Put it down to the rhetoric of the moment.

Still, the Cardinal did make a timely point. The Christian religion is indeed a religion of the Word, the Word of God proclaimed, explained, interpreted. But is it possible that Christianity has fallen into the hidden trap that threatens popular processes as we view them today: that if a thing is talked about often enough, long enough, by all concerned, all will come to a reasonable meeting of mind and purpose? This is not always the case.

It may also be said that the flood of meetings of priests, nuns, laity, resulted from centuries-old silence on the part of those religious estates. Priests' councils, sisters' organizations, parish councils chose this way because they felt that their voices had not been heard nor their counsel sought. Reasonably or not, some persons were convinced that the higher authorities had kept the dialogue within their own group. Others began such discussions because it was the response expected by Vatican II, which called for groups to consult, advise, weigh, consider the problems of the diocese. But the result: soon they grew weary, apathetic.

At that time Cardinal Heenan went on to add, "It is possible for us to be so exhausted by the number of meetings and discussions that we have no strength or inclination for the dull daily routine of pastoral life." "Dull, daily routine," those were his words.

In the Anglican Church, there is an old saying, "A house-going parson means a church-going people." To extend the Cardinal's thinking, it is the dull daily routine of house calls, hospital visits, visiting with and talking to people with humdrum, but real-to-them, problems, which is essential, but has been stopped because priests and religious are off to this or that potentially more rewarding meeting.

The matter became more complicated because dialogue and discussion did not necessarily mean success, accomplished goals, or instructed people. Meetings become polarized, few minds are changed, and sometimes there is little evidence of any educative process. More often than not, one meeting leads to another, speeches lengthen, and position papers ramble on. Talk today is highly inflationary; it takes longer to say less. Meetings produce more paper work, and paper "pollution." Church leaders stand judged on this: letters, forms, questionnaires, reports flow back and forth across the land, the offspring of the sociology of religion. Poll-taking is now an act of religion.

Cardinal Heenan noted two dangers in this present trend. The first: "paralysis by analysis." The Church, suddenly gone hypochondriac, was too busy taking its own temperature, checking its own pulse, studying its own symptoms. Meanwhile the message of the saving Christ goes unattended. The other danger was the reduction of the "Church" to another aspect of the world to be studied, analyzed, debated—but probably not lived by the very ones involved in the discussions.

In all this there is no advocacy of an abandonment of discussions or meetings. But here as everywhere: moderation. Bishops should be less anxious to get "programs" going which will involve endless rounds of meetings. Bishops, priests, religious, laity are to be aware of what Toynbee calls the "law of human inertia"—humans can only do so much in a day, and they wear out quickly. The Christian work, the dull daily routine must be done: signs of care and concern for one another in the niceties of human living, the helping hand, the time needed to reaffirm Christian love. One sad product of the new "religion by meeting" is a cooling off of Christian love. What may be needed is, as poet David Jones prayed, "Lord, redeem the time of our uncharity."

The other difficulty may have been a result of our American need to see big things, big changes, big solutions. Yet it is in little things that victory is won and salvation gained.

READING

In *A Hopkins Reader*, edited by John Pick (Image Books, 1966), one becomes aware of how much the poet loved the word "dappled." He uses it frequently in his poems and in his writing, as, "Glory be to God for dappled things." "Dappled" means spotted; or to reduce it to smallest terms, things which are not all of a piece, not all the same, which have marks of differentiation, ways in which we can tell them apart. Thoughts went from "dappled" to "little," "unimportant" things. Why is it difficult for us in America to praise God for little, insignificant, unimportant things? One of the burdens of American culture today is that everything must be boom or bust; any cultural item must be a hit or it is disregarded. We only want the greatest, the most, the best. If something is little or merely ordinary, it is rejected.

Have you noticed, for example, how often we use the word "hit?" We are told this movie is a hit, a "blockbuster." It is announced that this picture will gross the greatest amount of any film. The columnists announce that long lines are forming. What is hinted therefore, is it has to be good. Yet review the opposite side. The motion picture business is so terribly caught up in the money problem, it can no longer afford to have "small" movies. If a motion picture does not draw in two or three days, it is yanked out and replaced by a tried and true money-maker. But does this say by that very fact, that this motion picture is not good, that it has no value, and that it is not worthy of an hour or two of trifling with? Why not trifle?

Similar economic facts hold to the books. Best sellers. Why can't we have a least seller? Because it would not make great money. Does it remain a "least seller" because somebody thought it was not big enough? So they did not promote it enough to make the million. Yet if the book is a "hit" (no matter how bad), publishers line up to offer fabulous fortunes for the paperback rights. And then raise the price of the paperback to make up. There is no money to waste on "little" books.

This bigness fixation applies in almost any walk of life. An American meal is judged good only if it is steak. Does anybody like hash? A wine is pronounced the best if its price is high. Or if the savants declaim its *greatness*. Will anyone sing the praises of the insignificant little wine which just provides a nice background for an ordinary dinner? Ah, there is the key! Nobody wants the ordinary. It is dull, unappetizing, plain.

In fact, this theory can be applied to church matters. Liturgies must be great, big. Only the Sunday liturgy is worthwhile. What's wrong with a sleepy weekday liturgy of the priest and two or three early risers? Whatever happened to "if two or three are gathered together in My name?" Must every preacher be a Sheen? Every homily a gem? Every religious experience the equivalent of Paul being knocked off his horse on the road to Damascus?

Let's have dappled things, spotted in another sense of the word. They may be not all that great, but then they are not all that bad. We need those items which can please, without needing to provide us with ecstasy. Lincoln said: God must love the ordinary people, He made so many of them. G. K. Chesterton put it another way: The wonderful thing about the book of creation is that God clearly loves the minor characters.

So praise God for minor characters, minor events, for little joys and pleasures. In the long run they probably sustain and satisfy much better than the blast, the boom, the explosion.

In these contradictions what are we to do? Someone has proposed that the difference between the "old Church" and the "new Church" is that the "old Church" purported to have all the answers. The "new Church" (to the chagrin of some) claims not to have all the answers, or some (according to a few critics), but is now all questions. That may be a highly desirable development.

QUESTIONS

The Holy Rule of St. Benedict, speaking of the porter (gatekeeper) of the monastery (C. 66) says he must be a wise old monk, "who shall know how to receive and answer a question." Later, the Rule adds, "With all the courtesy of the fear of God, he should reply to a question humbly and with charity."

Laura Riding, poet, wrote:

> "What is to ask?
> It is to find an answer.
> What is to answer?
> Is it to find a question?"

Gertrude Stein, it is reported, on her deathbed was asked, "What is the answer?" Her last words were: "What is the question?" Shakespeare's Hamlet says, "To be or not to be, that is the question," but his answer at best was inconclusive.

NORBERT GAUGHAN

The question is a very mysterious human act. Logic is not happy with the question. As a rule the question does not make an assertion. It may or may not reveal something of the mind of the speaker, or of his ignorance. Again, the question is most important in philosophy. When Plato showed how Socrates, who knew the answer, used it to lead others to answers, he introduced the "Socratic method," still a good device to lead men to share mutually the discoveries of answers. The question is a way to lead others to find an answer, an answer which correct or not, may already be in the mind of the questioner.

Question and answer—they go together. Modern science would have us believe there are some questions we cannot ask. Back comes the philosopher: then why do we ask them? Why is there a drive within us to know the answer? Children are the best questioners. Their questions always begin with, why? Why this? Why that? Until the questioning begins to exacerbate and parents get exasperated and gruffly answer: "Because, that's why." But "because" is no answer of itself. "Because," as Aristotle hinted, leads beyond to a "be-causer." Jacques Maritain held that all men are born metaphysicians, that is, they keep wanting both to ask the question and find the answer.

Some questions today are not posed to find an answer. The mood too often is to cause anger, to disturb, to shake and move by the question. Which is a terrible thing to do to a question. The really true question is the one which leads those involved in the question and answer to find new truths about themselves, and about others.

It is a truism that in Brooklyn the ancient Jewish art of questioning is itself a standard answer—that is to say, a question is always answered with a question. Samples: Question: "How are you?" Answer: "How else should I be?" Question: "Are you happy?" Answer: "Is anybody happy today?"

Notice how Our Lord himself was a great questioner. It was in His dialogue, His questions, that He led others to discover truths about themselves and about Him. By questions He led many to make the act of faith necessary to discover Him. He asked His disciples: "Will you also leave Me?" Peter answered (Jewish style): "Lord, to whom shall we go?" Christ asked: "Who do people say I am?" And Peter eventually was led by God's spirit to answer: "You are the Son of the Living God."

The question is a religious act. The giving of answers is also religious if done in charity. No wonder, then, since St. Benedict's porter had to be both wise and old, it is as if Benedict were saying: to be young is to think one knows all the answers, so he may not receive a question well. The monk who is old and wise knows how to *receive* the question, and thus to answer it humbly and in charity. This gift should come with age. That it does not is an indictment on our times. To treat the question and the answer with love and respect is to respect both questioner and the giver of answers. Refuse to ask the angry question, the hurting question, the indicting question, the judgmental question.

Hasten to propose the humble question, the charitable question, the gentle question.

What else is a question but a quest? Our quest. The one we seek after is not some Holy Grail. Instead we search after Him Who made the Grail holy. He did that at the supper where the beloved disciple, reporting the dinner, said of Him, "Jesus, knowing that they were eager to question Him, spoke to them." And to their unspoken question He gave the gift of His living words in the magnificent Last Supper discourse.

Do not be afraid, then, to ask and answer questions of another. It is the way to discover His love in us and in the other; it is a path to meet Jesus, God's Question and humanity's Answer.

Part II

HUMOR
AND THE WORD

· In the change and turmoil of the day, one needs to keep a sense of balance, a perspective within history, and especially a sense of humor. This last particularly is essential for all true believers in the Church. Without it, we take ourselves, and our trifles much too seriously.

One point that is never satisfactorily answered is why the Bible never tells us Jesus laughed. The point is made that He wept. Yet nowhere does it report that He smiled or laughed. (The Gnostic "Gospel of St. Thomas" does do that.)

True humor can be read into some situations in Our Lord's life. This Lord of ours liked to play with words. Peter and John, fishermen, were told by Jesus their job description would change but not the title. They were "fishers of men." Our Church's foundation on Peter is based on a pun. Jesus said, "Peter, your new name means 'rock' and on this 'rock' I will build My church." That little pun has engendered monumental questions.

Laughter as a human activity in all the Bible does not come out well. *Proverbs* makes critical remarks about fools laughing. Foolish laughter will turn into tears. That laughter is healthy or good is never stated. Not surprising, then, that in matters of religion, the manner must be grave. The attitude, gait and dress of religious leaders, prelates, etc., is to be decorous. This allowed ordinary folk in the past to deride such attitudes by pointing out the foolishness of prelates, priests and monks. Example: the Bavarian scholar songs of the Middle Ages, the "Carmina Burana," mocked such men because they took themselves too seriously.

This antipathy to laughter in matters of state and religion was reinforced in our American tradition by customs arising from the Elizabethan, Jacobean and Cromwellean periods. The followers of Cromwell were a glum lot. (Would you be happy to be called Roundhead?) But the effect of Cromwell was to inject into the stream of religion the suspicion that laughter was somehow evil, unseemly, and even ungodly. Laughable things concern matters which are snide, low class, or scurrilous. High placed and highbrowed people would never be guilty of laughter. So, the work of such higher people (i.e., religion) is not open to laughter. What happens then? They take themselves, as well as their jobs, much too seriously.

Yet churchmen, or others who are supposed to be spokesmen for God or the things of God, must never take themselves too seriously. The Lord Himself continues to play some tricks on churchmen. Many a cleric who said, "I will never do such and such a thing," in fact was led by God and circumstances of history to recant, change his mind and do such a thing. If he cannot laugh about all this, that person is in trouble.

We're all taking ourselves too seriously. Have you noticed the decline of humor in our land? Not just in religious matters, not even in matters of government, but over the whole spectrum of our American life? It is easy once more to blame TV. The stand-up comedian, the one line joke, the bad, insulting humor of the variety and guest shows, have primed us to the easy laugh. The long and the humorous anecdote was not vindictive or malicious. It held up the human species and its foibles for all to laugh at. We have reached the nadir in humor, in nationality jokes, which are malicious, mediocre and uninventive. It is always easy to pick a scapegoat class. This gives us luxury to perceive ourselves as better than they. Priests comment on the absence of humorous stories at clerical gatherings. Mostly a few of the ill-mannered ethnic jokes sputter forth vainly. Absent now is even that ecclesiastical gallows humor—laughter at the foibles of bishops, pastors, of assistants, of parishioners, or religious. It was a way of really laughing at the clerical system. It prevented the cleric from taking life a little too seriously, and denied the conviction that salvation of the world depended on him alone. The priest too often conceives himself as Horatio at the bridge who must safeguard seriously the slightest insult to God's name or to His honor. Clerical trade repartee is dead; it's all too serious.

It is the same in the secular city. If it's not the dirty joke, the bawdy story on the banquet and testimonial dinner circuit, then remarks tend to be sentimental or just plain boring.

Humor in the pulpit has been discouraged as unworthy or without dignity. Yet read medieval sermons, where the preacher took great pains to identify himself with the people's culture. The sermons of St. Anthony, which he preached in the local dialect, are good examples of popular and humorous, but moving, talks. In the Renaissance and Enlightenment periods we met the elongated didactic sermon, particularly as it came from Anglican parsons and in super-oratory of the French preachers. Humor was discouraged (it made light of the things of God, it was said; it demeaned God). Humor prevented the poor folk from treasuring the things of God. This is unreal. It fails to appreciate the greatest wit of all: that God had to come down Himself, and as the Fathers of the Church constantly remind us, even stoop a little to reach our level to become one like us. Thus the joy, humor and wit of Christmastime, which should be with us all year long.

If we are never told, then, that Jesus laughed, still believe, He smiled then and smiles now. And He will smile, because He takes us seriously, especially our foolishnesses, strivings and failures. Smile, Jesus loves you.

Where to find humor? One place could be in our new words. If we are to have new things, new concepts in the Church, we are to adapt old words or create new ones. Alas, we have not risen up to the challenges.

NEOLOGISMS

That language is a constantly shifting, changing thing is clear to anyone who is concerned with usage of words and their meaning. New dictionaries and books on changing styles in language are always appearing. One such was the *Harper Dictionary of Contemporary Usage,* by William and Mary Morris, which generally got favorable reviews. The *Times Literary Supplement* of England, however, took a dimmer view, calling the book a "dilution of democracy" in language usage, and styled it "a dreadfully undistinguished book," lacking wit, subtlety and courage.

On the present abuse of "hopefully," the Morrises reluctantly allow it. But as the *TLS* reviewer, Joseph Epstein, well states, "The way that the misused 'hopefully' has come to function is as a secular substitute for the expression, 'God willing.' In place of religion, we now have bad grammar."

Thus religious bodies or practitioners do coin or reject words. In the interaction between religion and social sciences (sociology, psychology, etc.) some terms are adopted and introduced into a jargon of religion. As a temporary guidelist, until a more permanent work appears, we present a working word list for religion-talkers.

mini-Mass—any Mass lasting less than 15 minutes, no hymns, no homily.

macro-Mass—one which lasts at least two hours.

micro-mini-Mass—same as mini-Mass, except 9 minutes long, and no altar persons, no lectors.

homilese—type of language spoken by some priests outside the pulpit, especially in counselling or giving advice; liberally sprinkled with Bible quotations out of context.

support system—heavily upholstered and large chair for priest celebrants who are large and heavily upholstered.

over-kill—a homily or sermon over 25 minutes; also 3 collections on any Sunday.

jowl-to-jowl-confession—face-to-face confession in an extra small confessional room.

bottom line—"Did we make enough this Sunday to keep the church and school open this week?"

walkie-talkie—priest celebrant who is forever interrupting the ritual text with his own ad libs.

planned obsolescence—current American translation of the Bible.

alienated—a congregation which refuses to proffer any sign of peace.

vest-nik—any cleric who is excessively concerned with vestments.

peace-nik—one who stretches the sign of peace beyond 5 minutes for each person.

guided missal—any paper booklet with Mass texts to which priest celebrant tells where he is by referring to page numbers.

jet-set—that class of priests and clerics who boast of how quickly they can get any religious task done.

ecclesiastical plant supervisor—church janitor.

parish administration center dietitian—housekeeper in rectory.

oompah-Mass—successor to polka Mass; successful in German parishes; needs 76 trombones and 1 kettledrum.

panhandler—church usher; more properly, plate (collection) handler.

confessionette—old-fashioned confessional with middle separation replaced by small table to serve as confession room.

jaywalker—persons refusing to obey church traffic rules in approaching to receive Communion and returning.

natural selection—the habit or pattern of parishioners picking the same seating place in church each Sunday and resenting anyone who dares to sit in "their" place.

liturgimetrician—one who attempts to measure the total effect and impact of the Sunday liturgy, e.g., "Q. How was the liturgy today? A. Just so-so."

See also: homilimetrician, hymnometrician, and collectometrician (usually here, the pastor).

churchized—one who has been baptized, confirmized, Holy Communionized, reconciliationized, and collectionized, i.e., parishioner.

So a whole new field of coined, adopted, created, or to be created, words from other cultures and disciplines and the academic arena has been adopted to serve "churchese," i.e., church talk. Sadly, the middle management of parishes (priests, nuns, CCD'ers, etc.) are children of their generation. They borrow TV talk, ideas and attitudes. Whether the practice of religion serves the expression of faith, or is just another cultural phenomenon, is the issue. Right now, we bet the odds are in favor of culture. Is there faith? Yes, but you have to look hard to find it—hidden behind the jungle of jargon.

In time we can even introduce a new catechism help, a kind of alphabet for children of the new day.

CHURCH ALPHA-BITS

The English author Anthony Burgess in the *New York Times* magazine came up with a new alphabet with examples for our changing times. Since nobody in the Catholic Church has jumped into the breach to provide a similar item, here is a suggested trial guide. Herewith is an alphabet for the Church of the 70s. It could fit well into any proposed child's catechism.

A is for *Alleluia*, which in funeral Masses now replaces the old *requiescat in pace.*

B is for *Bishops*, who are either bad guys, boogeymen, or blessed Jobs (on whom descend all the calamities of the day). Individual choice picks which one of these the bishop is.

C is for *Communion in the Hand*, which is twice as good and enriching as any other kind. Or worse, as the pastor feels.

D is for *Doomsday*, which if you listen to some people in the Church, is always tomorrow.

E is for *Ecumenical*, which nobody can pronounce, few can spell, and might mean, "the money is tightening up, boys, so let's do some things together."

F is for *Foolhardy*—that is, any priest who tries to advise a nun about her lifestyle. Or her clothes. Or hairdo.

G is for *God*, who should not be mentioned in any discussions about the Church today. It is, after all, only a matter of structure.

H is for *Hair*, which any guru (including some kind of priests) must have in abundance to prove he is a prophet.

I is for *Inside Information*—that is, someone who met a Roman Monsignor on a plane and got all the dope.

J is for *Jesus Christ, Superstar*, prototype of new church music, successor to Gregorian Chant.

K is for *Kamp* (ecclesiastical type)—that is, any liturgical function which doesn't have at least fifteen priests concelebrating, it is not.

L is for *Lament,* which is a new application of the Scripture, "Where two or more churchmen are gathered together. . . ."

M is for *Mother Church,* in which there are an awful lot of Mamas' boys complaining.

N is for *Nausea,* which results from too many overripe liturgies.

O is for *Openness* in the new Church, which means anybody can insult anybody, and claim it is a part of the new freedom.

P and Q are for *Peace and Quiet,* which we demand so much and in the ensuing clamor destroy any possibility to achieve them.

R is for *Revolution,* which, it is claimed, is the way Jesus would solve any and all problems.

S is for *Sanctity,* which is even worse than bad breath in the morning.

T is for *Tradition,* which means anything that started yesterday.

U is for *Unbelievable,* and this is for some of the things we are told will happen in the Church in the 21st century.

V is for *Violet,* a liturgical color which is going out the way black went out.

W is for *Wide Open,* the way the liturgy of the future is proposed by some.

X is for *Xavier,* who used to be the patron saint of the missions. Since nobody cares for the missions anymore, Xavier may have to go, or become the patron saint of travellers, replacing Christopher.

Y is for *Youth,* in whose name all sorts of liturgical crimes are perpetrated by middle-aged adolescent priests, nuns and parents.

Z is for *Zzzzzzzzzzzzz,* the drone of apathy among most of the People of God while contending factions fight their personal hangups about the Church, Pope, God, etc.

On June 7, 1977, Pope Paul VI addressed the Consistory of Cardinals. The Archbishop Lefebvre affair was hot at the time, and the Pope defended liturgical reforms. But he condemned equally those who had taken liberties with liturgical reform and pushed their own versions and adaptations.

As that great sage and prophet Richard Nixon was wont to say, "Let me make one thing perfectly clear." Liturgical renewal is a good thing. But the amount of bad taste put into some of the personal adaptations could make you cry—or laugh. We prefer to laugh. Consider, for example, the following "styles" of post-Vatican II liturgies.

LITURGICAL STEW

When bishops meet, many good things happen, but there is one unhappy side effect. They tell each other ghost stories. That is, they try to outscare one another recounting the most horrible theological, liturgical, or spiritual excesses that happened. If their accounts are true, there were weird goings-on out there, particularly in matters liturgical.

These stories were not only reported by the bishops. Other Christians return from encounters, theological workshops, symposia, study weeks, alumni reunions, or conventions to tell about a peculiar kind of liturgy that took place while they were there. These hardy folk, not given to exaggeration, describe with blanched faces what took place here and there under the name of "the liturgy." Mostly these liturgies are performed by itinerant preachers, strolling monks, wandering religious, and searching seculars, who seek the new gospel of a meaningful liturgy, to be fashioned after the concept of a "Meal." The secret, clandestine, unauthorized, underground, huddled liturgies took place in cafeterias, convent lounges, dining rooms and kitchens, faculty meeting rooms, rumpus rooms, greenswards, leafy bowers, and bosky dells.

In a taxonomical vein, it is possible to establish a glossary of certain liturgies for future generations to identify them. These are some:

"The Stanley Kowalski Liturgy"—No, this is not a Polish insult. It takes its name from the hero of Tennessee Williams' "A Streetcar Named Desire"; Stanley, who strolled around the stage in an undershirt, yelling "Hey, Stella!" The main feature of the Kowalski Liturgy is the celebrant in a T-shirt, with or without a stole, who has decided to emphasize the homey, familial type, following the

Latin maxim "Utinam omne pendatur" (let it all hang out—including the tummy). At such gatherings, one expects a can of beer instead of wine.

"The Tiny Tim Liturgy"—Named after the former Syrian superstar, this liturgy features the celebrant who wears those velour, exotic white robes (not a chasuble, more of a white caftan), heavily embroidered. Since this is a hothouse liturgy for exotic types, the readings must be from that great Syrian mystic, Kahlil Gibran.

"The Al Fresco Liturgy"—Not named after a baseball umpire (that was Al Schacht), but rather because of its informality. The liturgy may stop and start at any given time. One celebrant drops in while another drops out. Halfway through, somebody decides they need something bready to break, and it could end up with crackers, matzos, bread, or bagels. It is all very informal to demonstrate the non-hassle quality needed for a meaningful liturgy in a hassling day.

"The Rod McKuen Liturgy"—This requires a celebrant who remembers that the gospel message has something to do with love, joy, peace and cats. Since the present Eucharistic Prayers do not mention these enough, this celebrant feels the need to improvise, which he does then and there. However, since his vocabulary is limited to little beyond those words, his liturgy limps. The "Rod McKuen" effect comes from what appear to be pregnant pauses, but which simply indicate the celebrant forgot what to say next.

NORBERT GAUGHAN

"The Lunch Counter Liturgy"—Another attempt at informality. The celebrant is dressed in
"civilian clothes," and everybody is seated around
the table, because that's, after all, the way the
Last Supper was. (Wait until they find out that according to the Jewish custom, the participants
were usually reclining on the floor with one arm
propped up.) The gifts are a loaf of bread from a
local bakery and the wine can be anything from
Manischewitz to Boone's Farm. The purpose, however, is to dramatize the unconventionality of it all.

"The Women's Lib Liturgy"—Found in areas of
feminist movements, high college degree areas,
some sisters' convents, where it is held that it is
only a matter of time until women are priests. The
entire liturgy is dictated by a few women, everybody says the Eucharistic Prayer, and readings
are from Kate Millett or Germaine Greer.

Some of these liturgies are still around; many
have disappeared. Why? There is one basic problem with all such liturgies—what do you do for an
encore? If "meaningful" means ever new meaning,
and that implies no more boredom and monotony,
there is a point of diminishing returns. (Liturgy
means "to celebrate," says one, and you can't
celebrate every day!) Or to put it another way, is
there a Keynesian law of liturgy: "Bad liturgy ends
up worse?"

Another reason for the decline may have been
enthusiasm and its natural consequence: boredom.
But it begins with good intentions.

MORE IS LESS

Was it not architect Mies van der Rohe who said "Less is more?" He was referring to the landscape littered with gingerbread-covered buildings, overdone with ornamentation. His solution: in architecture, do less. Or, when you overdo buildings with accretions and ornamentation, you wreck the effect.

Somebody ought to reverse the idea and give a course on "More is less" for liturgy planners. Like so many human beings who feel that if two pills are prescribed for the flu, four are better, some liturgy planners believe that if one or two things are allowed or suggested in a liturgy, why not do four or eight? Why not go for broke?

To help such a course, the following set of "More is less" liturgical laws may be useful.

1) *The Law of the Alleluia Inverse Ratio.* If one alleluia is a sign of joy, 30 alleluias strewn throughout the Mass in word and song, are better, right? Wrong. The more alleluias, the sadder the whole thing gets. So: if you are using 10 or more alleluias, watch it!

2) *The Law of Decreased Offertory Gifts.* If bread and wine are to be offered, the more people you get in the procession, the better. Correct? But the more people you get, the more gifts you need. So, at children's Masses we have books, rulers, pencils, etc. Need more children in the procession? Get more books. Get some pads. Need more adults?

Get some grapes. Better still, let each adult carry one grape. So it all becomes no longer "offertory" but circus; not "procession" but a caravan.

3) *The Law of Overdone Embroidery.* Get away from vestments, was the cry. Simplify, was the thought. No cassock, no amice, no maniple. But what happened? The alb got bigger; the chasuble more gilded, painted, colored; the stole came out of hiding and appeared on the outside, it grew bulkier, with more colors, and it and the chasuble became a kind of walking billboard ("Eat at St. Joe's"). More is less.

4) *The Law of More Songs, Less Music.* We need people singing. We need more music. Good. Let's really introduce it into the liturgy. So let's have music before the entrance hymn, and the *Kyrie*, and *Gloria*, and a post-First Reading meditation hymn, and a bunch of alleluias after the second hymn (see above), and an Offertory Procession song, and an Offertory hymn, and the *Sanctus*, and the *Agnus Dei*, and the Communion hymn, and a Communion meditation song, and a recessional hymn. Even though the instructions say, "This or that," optional means: let's do that too. Meanwhile, time is lost as one group stops, another gets ready, fastens the guitar, tunes up, etc. More is definitely less.

5) *The Law of Longer Prayers, Less Praying.* The "Prayer of the Faithful" was meant to be short, precise, and pertinent. Now the petitions have become advertisements ("Lord, help the pastor

pay the debt on the new church"), or sermons ("that we may all feel guilt whenever we eat non-union parsley on our potatoes"), or just plain wordy ("that . . . uh . . . we . . . uh . . . may . . . uh . . . hopefully look forward with hope to a future . . . uh . . . filled with good hope, for ourselves, and our children, and their children's children"). By that time, is it possible even God isn't listening?

6) *The Law of Longer Homilies, Less Wisdom.* A seminary professor used to say, if you can't move their hearts in 10 minutes, you move other portions of their anatomy. Sermons in the medieval and Renaissance period used to go on for an hour. This is one way the old Church and new Church still resemble each other. Homilies are as long as sermons, based on the thought that the more words thrown out, at least some will make sense. But here too, more is less, and the more ideas spewed forth at one sitting, the less retention.

7) *The Law of Excess Verbiage.* True, the celebrant is allowed to say a few words of his own at certain portions of the Mass. Yet there is danger of abuse from those who feel the number of their spontaneous words should exceed the number of Church fixed words. The "old" words are there because they are "formulae," time-tested. They are the ancient words of the worshiping community. But the greater the number of "spontaneous" words, the lesser the total impact. Few are all that good spontaneously.

On the Law of Decreased Offertory Gifts, the

situation gets worse instead of better, due to the growing number of people and gifts involved.

ACCRETION

There are liturgies and then there are accretions to liturgies. One accretion, presently happening as the Offertory procession, is something that the liturgical reformers never wanted, nor expected. It occurred because some people who do not understand liturgy wanted to embellish and dress it up. They thought the liturgical act by itself was not good enough. The accretion is a standard feature in a number of *special* liturgies in and around this area. It might be called "The Inflated Offertory Procession."

When it speaks of the Offertory, *The General Instruction of the Roman Missal* of 1970, which is the definitive voice in this matter, says simply (No. 48,1): "In the preparation of the gifts, bread, wine and water are brought to the altar, the same elements which Christ used." Notice that last phrase. It's important: "the elements which Christ used." Then, the Instruction (No. 49) continues: "The offerings are then brought forward. It is desirable for the faithful to present the bread and wine which are accepted by the priest or deacon at a suitable place . . . the rite of carrying up the gifts continues the spiritual value and meaning of the ancient custom when the people brought bread and wine for the liturgy from their homes."

The only addition of any "gift" allowed by the Instruction is this: "This is also the time to bring forward or to collect money or gifts for the poor and the Church. These are to be laid in a suitable place, but not on the altar."

Yet, what did result? A new ceremony, an inflated ritual, one filled with so much air and words, that instead of bread we get a liturgical souffle. Examples follow.

At the ordination of one bishop, flags were brought to represent his ethnic ancestry. Then came symbols of the work he had done—e.g., a globe because he was mission-minded, a moral theology textbook because he taught in the seminary, etc. Another case: at a recent ceremony in a convent, symbols were carried of the various works in which the sisters are engaged—secretarial notebooks, teaching texts, nurses' caps and the like. At an ethnic celebration huge rosary beads were carried by five children, a history book from the particular nation involved, records of music of the land, and so on.

That alone is bad. What goes with it is worse. Since these symbols do not of themselves communicate, their meaning being known only to a few, the planners of such liturgies think it necessary to add a commentary. This creates a new job for the liturgy—the person who interprets the meaning of the gifts. The added commentary is usually longwinded, extended and full of that highblown "churchy" language which in itself is

unreal. Sometimes the job gets complicated when
the commentator cannot coordinate the text on the
symbol with what in fact at that moment is being
handed over. Like a movie out of synchronization,
what is being recited at the lectern does not fit the
gift of the moment, which has either been given or
is yet to be given. The results sometimes are unin-
tentionally humorous.

Why is all this so bad? Because the act expresses a distrust of the elements that Christ used.
Bread, wine, water are common and cheap. We
need gold-covered things, nicely wrapped things,
silver trays, fluted glass, beribboned items. We
don't trust bread and wine. (Sometimes we even
hear ecclesiastical purple prose being read *about
them* by the commentator.) "Cheap" elements tear
down the dignity we are trying to proclaim. It all
resembles a kind of heresy; or it is akin to when
Peter said: "Lord, you shouldn't suffer and die"
(i.e., you are too great for that!). We say to God:
"You really don't know bread and wine and water.
Let's dress up the act for you, give you something
more and better!" We have renounced the pomps
of the devil, but we hold on to pompous displays.

It is we who do not know bread and wine and
water. We have not yet grasped the awe-ful implications of these simple elements. He who chose
this weak flesh of which to make an offering of
Himself to the Father, equally chose the plainest of
the plain—bread, wine, water. They were to be
the elements by which we are fed spiritually, by
which we are nourished and comforted and

strengthened. No pomps there. But humans cannot accept that. It's much too simple, unworthy, insignificant. Let's make of it a great gesture, a ritual parade. Let's praise ourselves and our works. Let's tell each other that we have gone beyond bread, wine and water, that we're special, and more, and above the rest, so we have done God one better.

This liturgical accretion is rather an excrescence, like a wart, or a boil. We want festoon and garland when the plain simple truth is— bread, wine, water—what He gave His Apostles. This is what He gives us so that we can give Him. When will we learn that liturgy is simplicity?

Simplicity, yes. Barrenness, no! The great wave of post-Vatican II renewal of churches resulted in a stripping of churches that has almost rivaled the despoiling of churches in the French Revolution. Our intent was good: to place new altars facing the people, to get rid of redundant and multiplied statues. But it did and has created a new difficulty—how to get "rid" of these things. Our suggestion: have special sales events.

SACRISTY SALES

These could be kin to garage sales and their grandfather, the flea market. The flea market originated in the open air markets in the oldest European cities. That's probably where the word "flea" comes from, with little or no weather protection, with all kinds of produce and vegetables, purchasers chose sales items and the fleas chose the purchasers. Or possibly the word "flea," which means something trifling, would apply to the kinds of goods on sale—mangy trifles, inconsequentials, not worth much. Garage sales are their local descendants. People, having searched their attics and basements, threatened by a flood of things bought but never thrown away, think they can get some money back. They relive the American dream that the dusty pitcher may turn out to be genuine Limoges, and the old painting a real Thomas Eakins.

For years dealers have been raiding old churches in Italy, Austria, and Germany. In the antique shops on First and Second Avenues of New York you will see their booty: brass candelabra, wooden statues, baroque cherubs; all at quite a cost. The Congregation of Clergy a few years ago was prompted to issue a warning about preserving "the patrimony of the Church"—that is, chalices, statuary, vestments, which had artistic or economic value. Some pastors did catch on to the collecting habits of the American public. One priest sold the bricks of his torn-down church for a good price because they were a special kind of brick now unavailable. Besides, they looked "old."

We suggest that parishes start their own flea markets or garage sales. These could be called "sacristy sales," cleaning up those overstocked sacristy cupboards of pre-Vatican II items no longer in use. In fact, letting imagination run rampant, we could come up with some good ideas.

Take those old, large and bulky missal stands made of wood or brass. Since many priests use just the Missalette on the altar, or some equally sleazy paper instead of a missal, why not offer missal stands for sale? They make lovely recipe stands for the kitchen or handy racks for do-it-yourself plans in the workroom. Or, if they're not too heavy, they can hold books for reading in bed.

Consider the thurible and censer. Most churches have done away with Benediction, and since incense is optional (thus mostly never used) at almost every other service, these could be turned to profit. Hippie communes would use censers since they're very big on incense. Offer them to your local mystics. These items are great for trance-inducing. Or on hot days, they might be carried along on crowded buses and streetcars to ward off evil spirits and effluvia.

Holy water sprinklers used to come in assorted shapes and sizes. Customers will grab them up and find strange uses for them, such as perfume sprinklers, basting utensils and the like.

Some priests no longer use ablution cups (they were for "purifying" the fingers after distributing Communion). People could use them as salt cellars, or individual finger bowls. Or for "dips" for potato chips.

There is always a good market in vestments. Priests who no longer use cassocks should think about asking some of their local seamstresses to make a few changes, add a few white stripes or other color stripes, attach a hood and sell these for caftans. Caftans are going to be very big (both ways) for many seasons.

There's also a surplus of surplices. (These are replaced now by albs for every occasion.) A little imagination can show how these can be used for some of the new style designs of clothing. Light, airy, flimsy, they could serve many purposes: baptismal dresses, etc.

Of course, candelabra are a big item. In most churches we are now down to one or two candles. The extra candle holders are reappearing in homes in great numbers as accent pieces, for candlelight dinners, and during power shortages.

It will take a little bit of ingenuity to find a use for the monstrance of old. Possibly good taste would demand here that we do not sell these items since they do have some sentimental attachment to the old-fashioned Catholic. For the young Catholic, who has never experienced "Benediction," there is no problem. He does not even know what it is.

Old Latin breviaries (any priest ordained twenty years has at least 3 or 4 sets available) can only be used as paperweights (they were very heavy), or even to line library walls as books "by the yard." Add to this the genuine Leonine edition in Latin of Thomas Aquinas' *Summa*, of which we gather there was a superabundance. The pages are usually uncut.

Prie-dieux, those kneelers that every church had before shrines (but since there are no shrines or statues, so no prie-dieux), can easily be converted into nighttime valets to hold change, keys, discarded clothes.

The clever pastor should certainly be able to turn these relics of a bygone day and outmoded practices into genuine money-making opportunities for his parish. We do warn that some sentimental types may take umbrage at possible "desecration." It is important to note that public relations come first here. Still, the priest who is saving such objects for the day when these will be popular once more may be living on false hopes. Their only future use now is souvenirs, nostaligic antiques, and remembrances. As the ad says, "turn them into ready cash!"

But objects were not the only items reclassified. Religious practices too fell by the wayside. There are liturgical and paraliturgical areas still untouched. Litanies have been sidetracked (or is it now "redlined?"). Possibilities presently exist to reintroduce both litanies and some forgotten saints.

NEW SAINTS

With the new Sacramentary (Mass Prayers) there exists a possibility of a variety of entrance rites. These may be refreshing changes from the standard ones used for the past number of years. The Sacramentary provides, particularly in formula No. 3, different invocations in series of threes, to fit any occasion; it further suggests that the celebrant may use other but similar expressions. The implication is that other kinds of invocations can be substituted. Further, in long processions, a lengthier litany may be adopted.

Unfortunately, some saints have dropped out of

sight through the liturgical calendar revision. Not
to pour salt on the wounds, people still smart that
we no longer have Philomena; Christopher has
been relegated to a doubtful memory. Many saints
no longer are even commemorated, let alone
memorialized. What could we substitute in litanies
for entrance processions?

In a helpful spirit we offer other possibilities.
Those invoked are not exactly saints, but they are
treated as almost-saints by their followers and
proponents. The proposal here is merely experi-
mental and a suggestion; it should scarcely be
thought to need any official approval.

The first proposed litany would be for social activists, social scientists, and for those who believe
that structure without dynamics (that's the modern equivalent of faith without good works) is
dead. This would be their litany:

Saints Input and Feedback, help us to communicate;

Saints Process and Procedure, show us how to
organize;

Saints Relationship and Meaningful, make us be
open to one another;

Saints Programmatic and Chart, demonstrate our
lines of communication;

Saints Biofeedback and Alphawave, let us become
aware;

Holy Martyrs Confrontation and Challenge, make us unafraid to cut down the idols of institutionalism;

Holy Innocents Personhood and Individual Freedom, pray that God's will be mine.

Prayer: All ye modern saints and wizards, our own creations of this day and point in time, help us to put down the shibboleths, idols and institutions of the past. May God and others be open to us to learn that we are newborn creatures with newborn tools and techniques for newborn ideas, all of which are not like any other ever before in the world. Amen.

The second litany could help those who oppose all the persons and ideas of the group above. It would fit Wanderers, Defenders of the Tridentine Mass, and "Bring Back Trent" groups.

Saints Status Quo and Good-Old-Days, take us back;

Saints Blind Obedience and Unquestioning Authority, pray that we may be the ones in authority;

Holy Men Cicero and Horace, teach all to understand that God speaks and understands only Latin;

Apostles James and John, "Sons of Thunder," lash out bolts of lightning at those who would dare to have Mass in any other way or language but the way God established in the Garden of Eden;

Holy Fire and Earthquake, destroy all churches which have altars facing the people;

Creatures Water and Bookworm, eat up, dissolve, wipe out all English sacramentaries and lectionaries;

Blessed Torquemada of the Holy Inquisition, destroy all those who do not agree with us;

Ye righteous bishops who burned Joan of Arc, help us rid ourselves of those who hear voices from heaven other than those we hear.

Prayer: God, it is good to know that you are on our side, and we hold you to the promise to destroy all our enemies. We are comforted to know that all who do not agree, be they popes, bishops, priests or laymen, are condemned to the fires of everlasting hell unless they recant, repent and side with us. Excuse that this prayer is not in Latin, God. As soon as we get a translation, accept it as a humble, sincere Christian prayer. Amen.

But, then, another litany would be needed. For those who believe the name "Christian" makes no monopolistic claim and allows them to seek other gods, beliefs or teachings, this litany may suffice:

Saints Buddha and Krishna, keep us in touch with ourselves, by touching others;

Dionysus, called "god" by the pagans of old, show us how to revel, celebrate, and experience continuous ecstasy;

Marcion and Basilides, and all you Gnostics, may we know how fortunate we are to be righteous, open, because of the secret knowledge we possess which other poor mortals have not;

Lilith, temptress, who the legends say led Adam astray, help us to experience each and every sensual pleasure;

All ye planets, members of the Zodiac, show us the times and the seasons when our stars ascend and our fortunes descend, so that we may live out our days in true astrology;

Blessed Paracelsus, master of Alchemy, teach us your magic and wizardry to change the base metal of daily life into the golden wisdom of how to enjoy life to the utmost each and every moment in the nowhood of our days.

Witches of Salem, Warlocks of Stonehenge, Druids of the Celts, make us open to the gods who live in nature that we may worship at their shrines;

Swamis, Gurus, and Holy Masters of Zen, Kung Fu and Tantric mysteries, aid us to divine the past and future so that we may be masters of the mysteries of the present;

Great Masters of Transcendental Meditation, guide us as we assume the lotus position, that our

bodies may be receptive to the flowing spirits of
the universe.

Prayer: God, we proclaim that Jesus is Lord. Still,
Lord, this does not prevent us from recognizing
other lords. Help us to turn to the East, West,
North or South to reach the God within us, to proclaim the God that is in everything, and to be all-in-
all with the great one Spirit who is in all things.
Amen.

The way religious practices are going in search
for meaning these days, these litanies probably could be expressions of some groups, styling
themselves Christian and Catholic. Naturally as
the community moves along to more splinterings,
to more esoteric gatherings, to more specialized
religiosities, the possibility must exist to be open to
newer ways.

Meanwhile, pardon, while we search the new
Sacramentary for a Mass and litany for times of
foolishness. Possibly that may be the one Mass
that is not in the new Sacramentary; it may be the
one Mass we need. The opening prayer might begin: "Oh, God, Who has revealed to us through the
Apostle Paul that we are to 'suffer fools gladly for
Christ's sake,' may we admit we are having a very
hard time of it these days. Amen."

Along these lines, in the new political awaken-
ing, another much needed liturgy can be introduced. One even provided for by the New Roman
Missal.

PRAYER DAY AGAINST BUGS

The New Roman Missal states that Rogation or
Ember Days are no longer fixed at a universal
time. Those were days of prayer and thanks for the
fruits of the earth and the work of men. Paragraph
46 says future Rogation Days are to be established
by national episcopal conferences, as needed
locally. The Missal (#47) states such days have
votive Masses, accommodated to the particular
needs. The U.S. Bishops thus far have not established such national days of prayer. A few
dioceses have made their own, but thus far there
are no *American* Rogation Days.

It could then be proposed that American bishops
should consider making June 17 an annual day of
prayer and thanksgiving, observed as the Memorial of the "Five Less-Than-Holy Burglars." It
should commemorate the deliverance of this land
through the now-famous Watergate bungled bur-
glary, and include all other wire taps, letter open-
ings and break-ins done in the name of good
government.

This is not to be a partisan feast, observed only
by Catholic Democrats. Thanks must always be offered for discovering incursions into the private
life of American citizens by all administrations.
We need ever to emphasize the duty of Christians
to suspect all public pronouncements of administrations, specifically in alleged national distress,
but particularly in election years.

Why not observe these on the patriotic holidays,

July 4th, Memorial Day? June 17 should be a "reverse patriotism"—the duty of Christians who love America and respect civil authority, but resist its encroachments into matters of religion, conscience and the spiritual.

We can propose a liturgy for that day. Watergate taught us all about "the bug." It began with the bugging of the Democratic National Headquarters, and led to knowledge of bugs on all the phones in the President's office. There were bugs upon key government officials by their superiors, and proposed bugging and surveillance by "White House plumbers" on all citizens. The Church, ever wise, has already provided a partial liturgy. The Roman Ritual (Father Weller's translation, p. 456) has a "Blessing Against Pests," which includes rats, locusts and all kinds of bugs. It begins appropriately with the antiphon: "Arise, Lord, help us; and deliver us for your kindness' sake," followed by an apt psalm (43-44), "O God, our ears have heard."

The first prayer asks God, ". . . even though we rightly deserve, on account of our sins, this plague of bugs, yet mercifully deliver us for your kindness' sake. Let this plague be expelled by your power." The second prayer continues, imploring God "before whom all creatures bow down in adoration" to "preserve us sinners by your might, that whatever we undertake with trust in your protection may meet with success by your grace. And now as we utter a curse on these noxious bugs, may they be cursed by you; as we seek to destroy them, may they be destroyed by you; as we seek to exterminate them, may they be exterminated by you; so that delivered from this plague by your goodness, we may freely offer thanks to your majesty."

A Mass on that day should have Nehemias (c. 8, vs. 1) as the first reading: "When the seventh month had come after the return of the Israelites to their cities, the whole people gathered, like one man, in the open space before the Water-gate. There and then, on the first day of the seventh month, the priest Esdras fetched out the book [of the Law of Moses] in the presence of a great throng of men and women ... and there in the open space before the Water-gate he proclaimed the law, before men and women and such younger folk as could take it in, from daybreak to noon, and all listened attentively while the reading went on." The Gospel might be (Luke, 12, 39): "Be sure of this; if the master of the house had known at what time the thief was coming, he would have kept watch, and not allowed his house to be broken open."

The penitential rite could include a litany of the special saints to be invoked. The following saints could certainly be called upon:

Saint Dunstan, patron of blacksmiths, to protect against break-ins;

Saint Matthew, patron of accountants and tax collectors, to protect against dishonest campaign fund-raising and distributions. He could also help against IRS harassment for enemies of the administration;

Saint Genesius, patron of actors, should be invoked against those who falsely come with disguises, different names and different identities;

Saint Alexius and *Saint Felix of Cantalicio,* beggars usually shown carrying bags containing money, could be invoked against bagmen and fund-raisers who seek to put on another kind of bug for heavy contributions;

Saint Lucy and *Saint Raphael,* patron saints of the blind, for the American taxpayer;

Saint Fiacre, patron saint of cab drivers, to protect against couriers who drop messages in side roads. offbeat highways, and the like;

Saint Vitus, patron of comedians, for the follies and comedies of our high politicians;

Saint Vincent Ferrer, patron of plumbers, could be invoked against White House "plumbers," and all "fixers";

Saint Raymond Nonnatus, patron of those falsely accused, can be asked to intercede for all who plead innocent;

Saint Catherine of Alexandria, Saint Ivo and *Saint Thomas More,* patrons of jurists, to protect us against young lawyers "on the make";

Saint Gabriel, patron saint of communications to deliver us from the deviltry of modern electronic snoops;

Saint Luke and *Saint Mark,* patrons of notaries, to guard against all false oaths;

Saint Michael, patron of policemen, against ex-policemen who join "plumbers" units;

Saint George, Saint Martin of Tours and *Saint Sebastian,* patrons of soldiers, against lying public reports from high military officials about the amount and seriousness of bombings in places we're not supposed to be, and in the building of newer and better bombs;

Saint Clare of Assisi, named in 1958 patroness of television, to help learn more about the inner workings of the state;

Saint Peter of Alcantara, patron of watchmen, should be thanked for the watchman who caught the "Five Less-Than-Holy Burglars";

Finally, we must not forget *Saint Nicholas of Tolentino,* patron of poor souls such as we, and *Saint Jude Thaddeus,* patron of desperate situations.

No irreverence is intended here. Whether the liturgy suggestions above are followed or not, does not matter. But should we not have some public day of thanksgiving and petition for the deliverance from the horrors of our modern supergovernment? Perhaps we should, if we will have learned from the present evils and done something about them. That question, sadly, is still open.

Newer situations create newer needs all over the place. Consider such an ordinary thing as greeting cards.

GREETING CARDS

A news item once spoke of new kinds of greeting cards on the market, brought about as a result of different social changes of our day, You are invited, for example, to send a greeting card to someone about to get a divorce, or to a person who just had a divorce, or to a father or mother who has just been awarded custody of the children.

Enterprising publishers of cards, especially those who publish for the Catholic market, should not hesitate to get on this bandwagon. There are many new occasions on which you might want to send a card to new people and new situations in the Church today. May we give you only a few? Others may wish to suggest variations. We expect no royalties and are doing this merely as a help for the social amenities in a Church experiencing changing times.

For the priest sporting a new beard: "Congratulations, Father, on the new addition to your face." (If the beard is full and covers from the nostrils down: "Thanks, Father, that new beard will certainly help your sermons; now they will be a little more muffled.")

102

For the priest who just shaved off his beard, having given it a trial from two to six months: "Welcome back, Father, we missed your face." Or, "We're glad you came clean; we always knew there was something behind that vegetation."

For the nun who has doffed the old style habit for the new: "Gee, Sister, you look great! Now join the rest of us in paying for our cleaning bills." Or, "What a surprise, Sister, we never knew you had legs . . . oops, limbs."

For the man elected president of the Parish Council: "Congratulations, and sock it to him—you know who I mean."

For the man retiring after three terms as president of the Parish Council: "Don't worry, you still have a few friends in the parish. I'm one. Maybe the only one."

From a Women's Libber to a woman appointed lay minister of the Eucharist: "Okay, we got you in the sanctuary; let's not stop there!"

To someone who has joined the charismatic movement: "Remember, it's not the prayer, it's the Spirit that counts."

To a young man about to go off to the seminary: "Everybody says you're signing on the Titanic; I hope you know how to swim."

For a priest who has decided to change his career and become a layman again: "Come on in, the water's fine. But remember, the pool's not heated and there are many sharks around."

For the associate pastor who gets his first parish: "Remember all those things you said you were going to do when you became your own boss? Take a tip, don't do them."

To a new lector: "You may be no Laurence Olivier, but then you're no Donald Duck either."

For the choir director: "Do you know any country and western hymns in Latin? After all, this parish is made of just plain folks."

To the new religious coordinator in the parish: "I hope you can put it all together. So far the priests haven't been able to do it."

To the deacon appointed for a summer assignment or internship in the parish: "Deke, you're unique!"

For the new parish cantor (leader of song): "Here's hoping you get to make your own golden record."

To the housewife becoming a CCD teacher: "Don't preach, teach. Then the kids will think you're a peach."

For newly appointed auxiliary bishops (there are more of them these days), we propose this one: "Desist, don't resist, just assist."

Probably not too many will seize this million dollar idea. Still, we only want to make the point that in the shifting positions, roles, offices and job descriptions in the Church, the people of God need a lot of patience, understanding and mutual support. If everybody keeps their cool, maybe we'll all stay out of hotter places.

How shall we learn of these new tasks? Maybe advertising will help. Now that the Supreme Court has declared lawyers may advertise their services, can the medical profession be far behind? And if they, what next?

ADVERTISING

Some servants of the people are now going to be allowed to advertise their wares. In the interests of consumerism and getting the best price, doctors and members of the bar will be able to publish advertisements in the newspapers, quoting prices and services. What a boon this will be! As we know, nothing false is ever advertised in the newspapers. And to paraphrase Mr. Flip Wilson, "What is advertised is what we gets." Maybe. Still, with the present penchant of some clerics, nuns and professional Catholics to seek the help of civil law in their dealings with Church authorities, can the day be far off when religious persons shall advertise about the services they can provide? This could be a real gift to the religious newspapers and magazines which are having a hard time getting ads. But better, it could help to identify for the public specific services by specific persons. With this thought we can all look forward joyfully to ads such as the following.

"Do you want eyeball-to-eyeball confession? Consult Father Truface who has the best set of eyeballs available in the business (recommended by Dr. Nogaze, eye specialist). Nothing held back. No truths hidden. No fees can be charged, by

Canon Law, yet some rental payment is reasonably expected for the use of the confessional room. Lower rental fees when the confessions exceed an hour."

"Want your marriage to last? Arrange to have the service performed by Father Tietite. His record is the best in the land. Of the 350 marriages performed by him in the last five years, only 70 have definitely broken up. Four out of five couples are thus satisfied customers. (Truth in advertising forces us to admit 120 of these marriages are pending in church courts.) Father Tietite guarantees also with each marriage a copy of 'How To Get Your Case in the Matrimonial Courts.'"

"For those in a hurry, come to downtown St. Ansgar's. Sunday Mass guaranteed to last no more than 15 minutes; daily Mass, 9½ minutes. Our Masses are geared to executives and people on the run: you, Mr., Mrs., or Ms. average hard working American type Catholic."

"Tired of that same old blah every Sunday? Have you tried the homilies of Father Syncere? No bible explanations, no politics, no do-it-yourself helpful hints. Father Syncere lays it on the line. He speaks middle Americanese. His diction has been approved by the American Association of Simple Language Users. Once you hear Father Syncere you will have had enough—to get you through the week."

"Are you unhappy with your present CCD teachers? Have they been giving your children that same old Martin Luther King, Cesar Chavez and Bluebirds course? Sign up now with the genuine article: the TRT (True Religion Tellers) School. We use the original Baltimore text (1890). Not one of our teachers is under 65. With each student enrolled you get a subscription to *The Ambling Catholic*, and *The Revelations of St. Ignota*, which warns what will happen if we do not all return to saying, 'Yes, Father,' 'Yes, Sister.'"

"Are you tired of those same old happy funerals? Are you disgusted with all those Alleluias? Enroll your loved ones now in the original and guaranteed 'Gloomy Special' by the Uriah Coughin Funeral Home. We guarantee a preacher who will speak in lugubrious tones and threaten hell fire for those in attendance who haven't been going to church. Ten weepy-faced ladies are also provided at strategic points in the church to sob out loud. No alleluia banners permitted. Original black vestments with maniple and coffin pall in black and silver provided."

"Unhappy with bible devotions, penance services, and esoteric liturgies? Come to our daily, all-year-round novena to St. Paraphernalia. Cures guaranteed. Weekly list of successful petitions provided and special cases entered into the second round of novenas. No nonsense prayers. Everybody kneels. No handshakes or signs of peace. Only genuine Catholic hymns (none of this new stuff) permitted."

"Outdoor weddings anytime, anywhere. Write to this secret Post Office Box number. (The local Bishop is tough and will not allow Masses except in church, so we must disguise our name.) We have had successful marriages on ski slopes, in an igloo, under water, on water skis, inside a hotel ice box (this was where the couple met), and other more unusual places. We will cater the marriage to suit your preferences and celebrant will wear appropriate vestments (ski suits, eskimo furs, scuba gear, swimming suits and fur-lined parkas). Remember: Father X is willing to oblige your extra-special wedding place desires."

Ah, but then we really don't have to advertise these days, do we? This is the joy of the present Church. Almost every such service is presently, or can be, provided by some cleric or religious. The names of these specialists are known to their followers. Word-of-mouth advertising works. Some old-fashioned clerics are unhappy because people do shop around. Worse, they are unhappy because there are some co-workers who will provide unorthodox services. If there are such complaints we must really take them up with God. It is He who has suffered such a diversity of religious types in our day. Almost any need or almost any expression of religion—real, imaginary or alleged—can be satisfied. Whether we are happy with it or not is irrelevant. It will probably continue.

Yet why stop at advertising in the newspapers, on TV, on radio? Certainly one of the newest ways to get your message, your logo, your insignia across, is by the T-shirt.

T-SHIRT ADS

Woody Allen tells the story of the Jewish clothing manufacturer whose whole new line of dresses was not moving. He prayed to God. In a vision God said to him: "Put an alligator on your dresses." "An alligator?" the dressmaker asked incredulously. "An alligator," said God. "Believe." The dressmaker did and his whole run of dresses sold fabulously. The alligator did it.

The reference, of course, is to the dress manufacturer, Lacoste. These shirts, dresses and clothing sell more; they have an alligator embroidered on the front. Since then there have been penguins, open umbrellas, and various other symbols, including initials, attached to clothing. They are all trademarks of companies which make money by giving you the great privilege to pay more to wear their honored emblem. This excellent (for them) idea was adopted for luggage and accessories. Louis Vuitton makes an expensive brand of luggage. The "in" thing is to pay scads of money for the honor of possessing luggage stamped all over with a design formed by the initials "LV." Then Mark Cross and the others got into the act. It is out of fashion to carry just plain old unimprinted luggage.

The final stage has been the proliferation of the T-shirt carrying messages. The sandwich-board man of old was a down-and-out bum who picked up a meal and a few bucks by walking around town wearing and carrying a billboard about the neck (hence, sandwich board), advertising "Tessie's Tea Room" or "Harry's Pool Hall." Nowadays people line up to pay for the privilege to be walking signboards, that is, to wear T-shirts with all kinds of trademarks, crests, insignia and messages.

Why can't parishes, churches, Catholic organizations, etc. do the same thing? Why not sell wearing apparel with messages? Could not the local altar boys' surplices be given free with the message, "Star of Jerusalem Incense?" Why should not choirs' robes be paid for by advertisements, "For your favorite hymns, sing along with the Paluch Missalette?" If we push it far enough, some vestments could even be paid for by being adorned in gold thread with the initials of the wine supplier (e.g., CBCBCB—that is, Christian Brothers).

Of course, the best source for both money and messages is the T-shirt. Old time Catholics may want a supply of T-shirts simply saying "Dies Irae" from the old Requiem Mass, while indicating the judgment of God to come.

Pentecostal groups could wear "Praise the Lord" shirts, and Tridentine Catholics could invoke the lost prayer (whose loss they think brought about the sad state of the Church), "St. Michael, defend us in battle," with an appropriate Michael emblem.

Benedictine Third Order groups could wear the motto "Ora et Labora," while Dominican groups could ask, "When did you last read Thomas Aquinas?"

Some Catholics who are certain that we are on the verge of declining as the Roman Empire did, could subtly hint the reason why, with a picture of the shattered stone tablets with the Roman numerals I to X, indicating the broken Ten Commandments.

Those who feel we have had too much talk in the Church and too little prayer could wear the emblem, "Expiation, not conversation."

Latinists who are optimists could wear, "Sursum Corda."

Liberals who have lost hope, who feel that Vatican II and its principles have been betrayed, could wear the emblem, "Bring back John XXIII."

Those who feel that only a good persecution will shock Catholics to their senses could proclaim, "Nero my God to Thee."

Nostalgia could work here. Why not remind us of those lovely hymns and poems that have disappeared, famous first lines, as it were: "Pange lingua," "Only God can make a tree."

The dimensions of selling possibilities are fantastic. Given the present need for money, our preoccupation with messages and slogans, and everyone's desire to stand for something, the Catholic T-shirt with matching motto would solve money problems at once.

Lastly, the messages could even be cryptic, known only to those "within." For example, use the old medieval prayer which said: "Keep the X; watch out for V; and observe II." Translated it meant: keep the Ten Commandments; watch out for the five senses; and observe the two laws—love of God and love of neighbor. As the TV hustler says, "Good advice! Get some today!"

Most needed of all may be what only a success-ful, dollar-oriented entrepreneur can provide—a booklet for sale in every Catholic Church in America about churches throughout the land, with descriptions of what can be expected in the liturgies by the Catholic traveler, especially for summer touring. Something like this.

MASS-ING OUT

Every local paper now has a weekly report on the quality of food and service provided by res-taurants nearby. Each man must know his terri-tory. For the most part, these local restaurant critics are gentle and over-kind. When they do en-counter a real bummer, they let the public know. Their negative judgments are challenged by people who have had other experiences at the res-taurants in question, mostly those who cook for themselves so much that their jaded palates approve any food anywhere as long as it's not their own production.

What many may not know is that a similar service could be just around the corner for churchgoers. Philbert Grave and his associate, Daphnilla Sobersides, founders of "Liturgical Analyses, Inc." have gone about the country reviewing Sunday liturgies in Catholic parish churches. Their appraisals are published in Catholic papers to guide those who seek more meaningful liturgies, less abrasive or Pollyannish homilies, and less tacky hymns. We provide a random sample of a few of their reviews to show you what is being done.

"*St. Engelbert Church, Washout, Texas:* This is a small, homey church which has three Sunday Masses. We attended the 10:45 a.m., the most popular. The decor was lovely, and the lectern was accentuated by a pink banner with a flamingo on it, urging us to 'Think Beak! Unless you can say good, don't talk.' Unfortunately, the priest who conducted the liturgy didn't follow that advice. His speech was halting, jumbled; the homily was an overlong warning on 'The Dangers of Ecumenical Communion Breakfasts.' (We are told that the associate, who conducted the 7:30 Mass is more a swinger, zips it right in there, and is great on timely subjects such as lettuce, slacks, and grapes.) Daphnilla thought the outfit the priest wore was a bit gauche, consisting of a mini-alb, and maxi-chasuble, on a super-maxi frame. She also thought the guitarist (this was a folk Mass) had a retarded finger, but musical selections were good, including that new country-style hymn, 'When We Gather in that Great Corral in the Sky.' The ushers were adequate, but the asking contribution ($2.50 for visitors) was a bit much."

"*St. Drusilla Church, Aposakee, Maine:* This is the only church in town; opportunities for Catholics to go elsewhere are limited. Daphnilla warns that kneelers are not padded, so girls, watch out for your nylons. The parish does not use the Missalette, but has its own prepared liturgy aid. Unfortunately it is printed on a 1932 mimeograph and is completely illegible, whether by design or not. The 11:30 Sunday liturgy had a handsome leader of song (looks like Sergio Franchi) who specialized in solos; the people sing only a refrain at the entrance and closing part. Seating is ample to match the congregation. The lector was a twelve-year-old boy who had problems with the Epistle (St. Paul on debauchery, etc.). The parish has fourteen people to help in giving out Communion (the Communion service took only three minutes). The pastor, a monsignor who obviously has a 'bigger job' somewhere else, spoke down to us. Still, his subject, 'The Processions in the Holy Trinity and Modern Application,' couldn't lend itself to much understanding. The women ushers lent a beautiful touch, and Daphnilla reports that in their uniform—Pentecost Red blazers with gold buttons and skirts of Blackwatch plaid (there are many

Scots descendants in the parish)—they made an attractive display when they massed in the front to take up the collection. Strangers are invited to take part in the Offertory Procession, and for $3.50 can get a document testifying to the event as a souvenir."

"*St. Uncumber, Uneeda, Pennsylvania:* This is an inner-city parish with an auxiliary bishop as pastor. He is usually not available (he has the 6:00 a.m. Mass on Sunday). The staff is made up of visiting and foreign student priests, with one interning deacon. The 11:00 a.m. Mass is always potluck since the celebrant changes weekly, allowing a variety of possible liturgical styles and sermon techniques. The loud-speaker system dates to 1943 and keeps fading in and out, which creates interesting and unintended snatches of theology. Music is provided by Miss Willamette Norngro, organist since 1930 (she also is sacristan and her flower arrangements specialize in plastic). The priest does all three readings. The 11:00 a.m. Mass, with homily, is usually finished in 23 minutes (an advantage to Sunday-brunchers). There is an entrance fee (pew rent) but it is minimal. Daphnilla reports that Miss Norngro's repertoire is limited, and on one Sunday she did break into snatches of the 'Dies Irae.' Still, the time advantage outweighs all else."

Why all this? To remind you of one sure thing: the "one" Church is pluralistic in celebration. It suffers (that's the correct word) a variety of liturgies. Little wonder people are "shopping" for Sunday Mass. Pastors try to invoke the "you belong and must attend this parish" law, but a good portion of church-goers are trying various parishes. Priests may resent this and complain of their "brother" priest who is undercutting them by providing other services and liturgies. Yet it is a fact of Church life today.

Speaking of liturgies, have you noticed how the newer hymns have become more personal, more emotional? One thing we have not yet introduced into Sunday liturgies are madrigals.

MADRIGALS, TRUE AND FALSE

In the last decade there has been growing interest in recordings of that musical form called "madrigals." The renewal has been due to some creative scholarship, the discovery or re-editing of lost manuscripts, the willingness to recreate and use medieval and early Renaissance instruments, and new musical groups that make this lost musical heritage a delight of discovery.

Madrigals probably were developed in Italy. The works of Claudio Monteverdi and Gesualdo are among the best-selling classical discs. When performed by choral groups such as the Purcell Consort or Grayston Burgess and his consort, they provide hours of enjoyment. There is also the music of Josquin de Pres, a Flemish composer. All such research has even led to amateur and professional performances of madrigals in concert halls. We occasionally encounter the madrigal, but in the form of Christmas carols. Yet madrigals were to go beyond that.

Would it surprise you to learn of newly discovered madrigals? We are happy to present them here, to show how the madrigals may be in keeping with some of the hymns we are singing today in popular liturgies. For example, we are proud to present for the first time here the madrigal, "Oh Happy Meal," by an Italian unknown. The text is as follows:

"Oh happy joy, oh happy day.
To eat with Jesus, tra-la, tra-lay.
What fun to gather, what fun to play
At being Christians, tra-la, tra-lay."

Another hitherto unknown one from the medieval French is called "Happy Talk." The French author is Noel Diamant.

"I talk to the tree for it is my brother;
I talk to the sea for it is my mother;
I talk to the stones for they are my friends;
I talk to myself and that never ends.

I talk to Allah, use the Koran too;
I talk to Krishna and Buddha too;
I talk to Jesus, my friend and lover;
For best of all, He's like any other."

A longer madrigal comes from the ancient Flemish, by one Rodrak de Kuen. It catches much of the piety of a few of our newer and friendlier liturgical hymns:

"By wood and stream I follow my dream.
In mist and sky there am I.
Speak not to me of vile men,
Whose lives in cities are as a pig pen.
Nay, my friends are those whom God's Spirit
    chooses:
No sinners, no wicked, nor one who boozes.
Together we friends walk by the side of the sea,
Wherein all spiritual things do we agree.
Our talents so great are gifts from above,
Special signs for us whom He truly doth love.
Let others have hungers, fears and their doubts,
We are God's chosen; they, miserable louts."

Of course, we joke about such madrigals. That these homemade inventions sound much like what passes for certain hymns in "nature" Masses today is sad. The composers of the madrigals knew that the romantic song, the secular song, had no place in liturgy. They sang their song of lost loves and tears for love unrequited at dinners and banquets. But in their liturgy, clear, true, honest, unsentimental theology prevailed. Their church hymns had words that were honest and sincere. They did not at all reek with that self-adulatory treacle that passes for liturgical hymnology in some churches today.

Madrigals were sentimental; hymns were not. Hymns had theology; madrigals were romantic. Where theology and madrigal were wedded, as in some songs at Christmas and Easter, there was no foolishness, no "we are Sons of the Sun," and how great it is to be "jogging with Jesus."

We return to a theme that must be insisted upon: until our liturgies go back to good hymnody, not the "walking with the wind, climbing the mountain, feeling God's breath on my cheek" kind of song, but "The Old Rugged Cross," "Lead Kindly Light," and matters of that kind, our hymns will be failures. Why? Because they are out of touch with the real world, and with a Christian theology of the world.

Another "what is needed" suggestion is a good liturgical team in each parish.

TEAM LITURGY

Now everything is team: from surgical team, team of salesmen, news team—that's it. Churches have team ministries, parish teams, pastoral teams. Consider the news team, the "good" news team. Since daily news is such a bore, one thing after another, we've subdivided news and have a team of experts: for weather, for sports, anchor man for general news, one for local news. It's too much for one person, but teamwise it can be handled.

How about a Sunday liturgy team? Could it be that some day at our parish church we will be first greeted by our anchor man, the commentator, thus:

"This Mass is being presented by our liturgy team. It is my task to weave together the many strands of the liturgy to create one meaningful experience in the praise and worship of God. Today," he continues, "you will hear Blossom Jones, our outstanding Responsorial Psalm Specialist. Blossom, acclaimed in many churches for her fine recording of 'The Devil Made Me Do It,' will lead us in the meditation song, 'Rejoice All Christian Persons.' Our choir director, Theodolph Gutzman, specializes in lugubrious music and will make us happy with his 'Ode to Death.' Theodolph has a Grammy Award for his record, 'The Joy I Get When I Cry.' For today's Mass Theodolph promises us a truly sad time, a melange of tears, sorrow and even a bit of nausea.

"About our priest celebrant, I have bad news and good news. Our regular celebrant, Father Eustace Van Stroheim, who whips us all into one in his Teutonic style, has been called to coordinate the free-floating parish of Martin Kennedy Roncalli at Kenosha Falls, Vermont. He has been sent there by the Vatican because only he, according to Vatican judgment, can bring order out of the chaos there from experiments in combining the Coptic, Mozarabic and Roman liturgies with country-style singing.

"Comes the good news. Our team liturgy is proud to have Father Linsdorf Meyer, a former

Southern farming country confirmationist preacher. As you may not know, Father specializes in homespun, down-to-earth, old folk type liturgies. Thank God we have no smart types and Ph.D.'s in our parish, so we can enjoy Meyer at his finest. He will deliver some insights from his years of sharing, giving and fellowship, while he lays it on the line about hell-fire and damnation.

"Next we present our organist, F. Energy Smalls, featured on our magnificent calliope organ, only recently acquired from Olympic Amusement Park (now closed). He will play, full diapason, the recessional, 'All Ye Carrousels of Heaven Praise the Lord.' He will be assisted by Mischa Euer, former choir director for the Pannonian Orthodox Church, now serving as a representative of the Inter-Ecumenical Agency for the Return of the Ancient Bessarabic Chants. Mischa has promised to open with a bang and lead us in the lament of the departing Byzantine soldiers at the fall of Constantinople in the 15th century, 'We Told You To Do It Our Way.' After the sermon—I mean, homily—R. Jeffrey Theobald, head of the financial committee of our parish council, will make a special appeal. The council would like to alert you to a few important facts about the future of our church, our school, our country and our world, which will take only a few minutes. Then we will have our annual appeal (it's not a collection) for the preservation of the original guitars used in our first folk Mass in this parish in 1962.

"Oh yes, serving you today at the altar are

Spikey Farhart and Mimsy Stokes, our altar boy and altar girl (shall we rather call them 'altar persons?') who received their diploma in the 'Liturgy Seminar for Little Persons,' conducted by our diocese. They graduated *summa cum laude* in not tripping the celebrant and water pouring. Last, but never least, is our perennial deacon, Ramsey Slipoff, who is in his third year in the seminary as deacon. He has been held back from priestly ordination for his failure properly to interpret the wishes of his field representative at the seminary. Let's show Ramsey we don't worry about those silly things by giving him a vote of confidence. When the time comes for him to say, 'The Mass is ended, go in peace,' let's all get out of here as quickly as possible.

"This liturgy is carefully planned and must take a little extra time. You understand that. So the twelve o'clock Mass, which usually follows this one, will now begin at one in the downstairs church. There are telephone hostesses available to call your relatives in case you are expected home for dinner. It's worth it, for we want to give you a liturgical experience and we are proud to say this liturgy team can do it. In fact, we really like to give it to you. Thank you, relax and enjoy. May this liturgy bring you closer to each other—and oh yes, to God too."

An hallucination? Possibly that's where we're headed. Given the team effort, the need to get everybody represented, and that a one-person liturgy may be simply repetitious (some old hymns and a sermon), we can move in the direction shown by TV. Bring in that folksiness and down-to-earth holiness (like that sausage that comes from down on the farm). Forget about the liturgy being devotional or praising God. In the new Church we've got to attend to many egos, strange and diverse talents which ordinarily would not be considered. Now they must be used (participation is the name of the game) for God's people. The decade ahead promises to be thrilling. Liturgies will become less community prayer and more a place where specialists only can gather, do their thing and make us all captive audiences while they perform what they think liturgy is about, even if we don't.

Ah well, the real problem is that other things have changed too. And the change, instead of helping, has just made church life that much more complicated. Consider the problems of decision-making. Exercise your imagination; together let us wonder aloud what might have happened if such processes were used in the past.

DECISION-MAKING

There exists a legend that Pope Leo the Great stopped Attila, leader of the Huns, at the gates of Rome about 450 A.D. How did the legend start? In view of the nature of the decision-making process at the highest levels today, could it be that the reason Attila never entered Rome was because of the following?

123

Attila with his mighty army stands at Rome's
gates to enter the city. The vested Pope awaits,
ready to forbid him. Then from within the city a
messenger bursts forth. To the Pope he says,
"Could I see you for a moment, sir?" Leo, surprised, steps aside to confer with the messenger,
who says, "I have a letter from the Roman Cardinals. They fear that you are not going to be
strong enough with Attila. It is not enough merely
to forbid his entrance. Point out to him that he
must make a declaration of errors, submit all his
writings to us for review. We will examine them
carefully, list the errors they contain, and forbid anybody to read them, lest their minds be poisoned."
The Pope is surprised, since to his knowledge
Attila cannot even write. He moves to Attila, when
once more he is stopped by a tug at his sleeve from
one of the popular priests of Rome, who says, "Sir,
before you make this important decision, could I
have a few words?" The Pontiff grudgingly agrees,
and in a private place, hears the priest say, "Sir, I
know you are thinking only of the good of the city
of Rome. You must also think of the good of the
whole Church. If you move in this matter you may
be setting a legal precedent which will destroy all
Huns forever. Yes, they are barbarians, but too,
they are God's creatures, equal to us. They have as
much right to live in Rome as we do. It is possible
that their ancestors occupied this land before we
came upon the scene. I speak for the priests of
Rome, in solemn council met. In the name of the
civil and natural rights of these barbarians, stop
and think. Let them occupy the city. We are confi-

dent we can work out an amicable agreement on the basis of peaceable understanding." While Pope Leo thinks this hope is a little presumptuous and naive, he does pause to consider.

Another interruption comes from a group of priests who approach to say, "We are the organization committee of 'The Priests of Europe.' At our meeting we passed a few resolutions for consideration before papal power condemns this simple-minded barbarian." The leader, a Hibernian by birth, continues: "This is a time in the Church when one man can no longer take upon himself weighty decisions. In the charity of Christ, and as our duty we have decided to help you in this matter. Before, in deep humility and only searching for truth, we had commissioned two study papers: the first report is from one of the barbarians on 'The Needs and Rights of Barbarians in Their Policy of Subjugation.' I may tell you this is extremely interesting and well done, with manifold references to some of our modern revolutionaries. It is also well documented and is based on the new theology of subjugation, which we feel is founded on the Gospel. The other, 'The Theological Implications and Aspects of the Catholic Culture in Conflict with the Barbarian,' is by one of our leading journalists, who is only incidentally a priest. This well-researched paper points out that Catholics of Rome have no right to move unilaterally in this matter and should first consult in collegiality with all the priests of Europe. In a spirit of ecumenism, we should also hear our heretical brothers, the Gnostics, the Donatists, the Pelagians. Lastly, we agreed in the spirit of healthy neglect, it might be better if this whole issue were tabled until we could consider it together with you and your bishops at a plenary assembly to be held next year. Could that meeting not be in Rome but possibly in Constantinople? We understand the facilities there for visitors are much better than the Roman hotels."

The poor perplexed Pontiff pauses in puzzlement. He is getting more advice than he needed. In an unchristian mood of stubbornness, he is ready to do as he intended, to forbid Attila entrance into the city. Yet once more he is stopped, when a stately, imperious woman, obviously a person of prestige and learning, comes forth speaking as the Chief Person of the Order of Deaconesses of the Church of Rome. She prefaces her remarks with the biographical note that she had lately attended courses at Egyptian University of Alexandria. Here she has found great wisdom and understanding from nonchristian professors. As she tells the Pope, her doctoral thesis was on "Xanthippe, Wife of Socrates and What She Taught Her Husband," which has been adopted as a textbook. The lady then chides the Pope for being a male chauvinist who has not taken into consideration the advantages of life in Rome for the women of Attila's party. In Rome, these women would be able to find new jobs and tasks in Roman society. In time they could even become members of the Senate and possibly the College of Cardinals (not all of which were priests).

The disgusted Pope tells Attila: "Take it. You can have the city. It's yours!" But the wily barbarian leader has not risen to his position by accident. He has been watching the scene and hearing the dialogue, with the free advice the Pope has received. Attila speaks: "If that's the civilized way of doing things, no thanks! If the man in charge of this city has got to go to all those meetings and cannot act without the approval of every single person, this city will soon fall." So Attila, without consultation with any of his people (remember, he was a barbarian), marched away. Weary and sad, Pope Leo returned to the city to attend a protest meeting scheduled at St. Peter's by the followers of the movement for "A Return to the Etruscan Language." It had been arranged that the official artists would paint the scene when he was pelted with ritual books in modern Latin. Such paintings were to be sent to all the provinces to demonstrate how free opinion in Christian Rome did not stop at attacking the Pope.

So that's how Rome might have been saved. If it was saved.

A while back we mentioned the subject of the disappearance of some saints. That still troubles many Catholics.

21ST CENTURY SAINTS

It is more than a decade since certain saints of old were "demoted." Last reports are that Christopher and George are still hanging in there. The reason for the "downgrading" of these, you remember, was that accurate historical information about them was not available.

As a service to Christians of the 21st century, and to make certain that some contemporaries of ours who now exhibit truly heroic virtue will be properly honored at that future time, we present possible saints for tomorrow, with appropriate biographical data.

First, there is Blessed Hibernicus, the true theologian of the 21st century. Born at Bad Mouthing on the Pope, this scholar received his theology degree at the age of seven, with subsequent degrees in just about everything else by the age of 21. In a series of highly (commercially) successful books, he developed his theory of "Shared Responsibility for All, but Theological Interpretation for the Chosen Few." Although a priest, because of his extreme humility he has renounced the clerical garb because he feels unworthy of it. He has, however, kept the royalties from his books, so that he can leave the money, as he says, to the poor, when he is called to that great Classroom in the Sky. Death holds no fear for him, since he has it all figured out and there will be no surprises. And somebody else will pick up the expenses.

Next, we must remember Holy Jocunda, the American woman foundress of the religious order, Devotees of Fun, which was extremely popular in the 1970s. At first, embracing the traditional religious life, Jocunda had a vision while working among the recently impoverished at Las Vegas. It was revealed to her that it was more fun losing her own money at the slot machines, and so she foreswore her former vows to take on herself the truly revolutionary vow of service to the jet-set, beautiful people. Jocunda believed that her daughters should emulate these chosen few, so that the lonely souls would receive comfort and encouragement. Jocunda died at Fun Villa, her religious home at Biscayne Bay, at the age of 35, worn out in the service and ministry of fun.

Who can forget Venerable Neuter, the man who was angry with God because God hadn't allowed him to be born vari-colored, and of mixed ethnic background. As Neuter used to say, "I want to know and feel what it is like to be red, yellow, black; Irish, Italian, Polish, Jewish, German and Arab, and so on!" To offset this handicap, Neuter developed his theory of spiritual camouflage. Basically it was this: whenever people were gathered together, Neuter waited until he found out what group was in power, or in control. He then adopted the stance and attitude of every other minority. By this, as he said, he could give witness to the absence of these groups by his protesting presence. Neuter developed his doctrine so well that at his death, no one knew who it really was who had died.

We should pay tribute to Blessed and soon-to-be-Saint Cinema. This enterprising young man believed sincerely that God had missed the boat in not arranging for the scriptures to be done first in movie form. "The film," Cinema used to say, "is more potent than the word, and the word must become Supermovie before it lives." Cinema (who took as his confirmation name, De Mille) believed that churchgoers of the future should insist only that all believers attend pre-selected flicks which would dramatize the conflict of good and evil. Young Cinema authored, directed and produced the mammoth film (it took 7 days' consecutive viewing to see it in its entirety), "The Hollywood Gospel." He also produced "Godzilla Meets Race Hatred," "The Beast from the Affluent Society," and "Beach Blanket Girls at Sodom and Gomorrah."

There is the Reverend Liturgicus, devotee of the cult. Nothing was wrong with the world, this holy man felt, that could not be set aright by the proper combination of ceremonial, celebration and meaningful rite. Liturgicus spent all his years (unsuccessfully) searching for the proper combination of these elements. He had passed beyond the organ and guitar as liturgical instruments and felt that the liturgy of the future had to take sharp notice of the marimba. Liturgicus authored many special hymns for the new liturgies, including "Give Me That Old Sign of Peace," and "We've Got To Chant Together If We Want To Stay Together." Liturgicus favored rituals for small groups, and was working on a "Celebration for Midgets," when he died from an allergy caused by overexposure to liturgical banners of contradictory materials.

We would surely fail our duty if we failed to pay tribute to that most modern of all to-be-saints, the Hallowed Whiney Moaner-Groaner. This well-known person was the most typical of 20th century churchgoers. His presence at any gathering of the blessed was punctuated with tears, sobs and whimpers (his). He claimed that his mission was to remind all that man has no lasting place here on earth, which was meant to be a vale of tears. He proved both of these claims by his constant carping, continuous criticism, and careful caterwauling. It is said that by his death at 69, he had shed more tears of complaint than were ever poured out by all the people at the Weeping Wall in its long existence.

Doubtless there are other modern candidates for sanctity, but these will suffice. As we said, the record of these present great men and women should not be lost to the future. If then they ask whether we 20th century believers were saintly, they can point to the examples of those above and say, "With such people around, the rest had to be saints—or else crazy."

Yet we must be aware that the current mood is not amenable to saints or their life stories. Even if, let us say, a religious classic were in the offing, it would probably not get printed. The parlous state of religious book publishing is the problem.

HELPING THE OLD BOOKS

No religious books appear on the best seller lists. Why? The Bible is always a best seller. What about "religious" books? Billy Graham's *Angels*

131

was a popular item; it appeared on the list because the publishers took their own polls and proved the book was a best seller. The publishers of "the list" claim religious books are for specialized audiences, so they are not *popular* "best sellers." Even if they outsell those *popular* books.

We suggest another reason. "Religious books" do not have the spice and extra pages of purple prose that in our day make hack writing become a best seller. How many best sellers of the past decade have survived? Anybody writing a "religious" book to be a best seller should remember this.

If some of the famous religious books of the past were to be published today, the authors might take heed of the following.

Bishop Augustine of Hippo seeks the opinion of a publisher about his book, *The City of God.* The editor advises thus: "You have a potential hit, Gus, but it needs work, a lot of work. Take the title. Who's going to buy a book called 'The City of God' today? Let's face it, God's not 'in,' the devil is. You do mention the city of men—wait, I have it! Let's call it 'Sin City,' just 'Sin City.' That is the city of man, isn't it? Wow, 'Sin City' bound in red and purple, and big letters! Hey, Gus, as a bishop you're a safe citizen. But we all know about your wild youth. Could we get a painting of that old girlfriend of your younger days, the one that you married and got rid of? That painting on a red jacket would sell millions. Let's subtitle it, 'Former Sinner Tells of Life in Sin City.' We could get three million just for the paperback rights!"

Thomas Aquinas seeks help for his *Summa Theo-
logica*. His literary agent knows no book called
"The Highest Points of Theology" would sell. He
tries to sell Thomas thus: "Tom, this is a strange
book, not enough potential to be a best seller. We
have to sell more than theologians, who always
want free copies anyhow. Let's get to the public
market where the dough is. Could all this be cut
down? It is already cut down? Yeah, but there's a
lot of stuff in there the average guy doesn't need to
know. Get rid of all that virtue stuff, concentrate
on the vices. How about all this on the Blessed
Trinity? That's not a hot item today. But keep the
Spirit in, we can sell those charismatics and
pentecostals; they've got money to spend. Could we
get a new title? With all your stuff on anger,
violence and sex, Tom, how about calling it 'The
Joys of Violence,' or 'The Rewards of Sex,' or
'Violence and Sex Are Natural, Enjoy It!' That
could get you on the talk shows. Oh yes, all that
weight you're carrying around . . . well, maybe TV
spots and radio phone-ins. You are too fat for a
good picture. You have an old photo when you
were skinnier? We don't want anybody to mix you
up with William Conrad and 'Cannon.' Hey, that's
it! How about 'Tom Aquinas and the Crimes of
Man'?"

A book publisher tells Thomas a Kempis his *The
Imitation of Christ* needs some reworking. "I like to
meet a man trying to make humans better. There's
something in your book, Mr. Kempis, that grabs at
the heartstrings. Still, can you take some construc-
tive criticism? This book should get to as many

people as possible. We really don't care about the money. It's just that we want to get to the ordinary Joe and Jane, don't we? Drop that 'The Imitation.' Nobody wants imitations, they want the genuine thing. Oh, there's only one genuine Christ, huh? Well, how about a 'know-how' book? There you go—'How To Be Your Own Christ.' Those 'how-to' books do well. Or maybe, 'Ten Easy Steps on How To Be Your Own Christ.' Clean up the flowery language. Piety turns people off today. Get tough. You gotta hit em hard, you gotta punch em, and you gotta sock it to em. 'Be Christ, or else go to . . .' How about that?''

Ignatius of Loyola approaches an editor with his *Spiritual Exercises*. He is greeted sadly by the editor, with these words: "Iggy, I admit this is a good book, a great self-help book. Maybe you have too much hell-fire and damnation in it, but that's a matter of taste. Some people like that stuff and we can sell it. But your whole approach is wrong. You can't talk about 30 days of spiritual exercises. Nobody has that much time to waste on that stuff. Can we get it down to seven days? Or better, seven hours? Look at today's book hits, 'Self Improvement in 30 Minutes a Week,' 'Exercise to Health in Five Minutes.' And you want a whole month! Times are different, Iggy. People need cruises, vacations, and that takes all the spare time. Look, speed up your timetable. If you don't do any better, let's go for seven days—'Seven Days to Heaven.' How about that? You don't like that? Mr. Loyola, in this business you have to compromise. Go home and think it over. Don't wait too long, cause I have another hot item here—*The Joy of Speedy Sanctity.*"

Since the copyrights on all these books are dead, an enterprising person could rehash these classics. If the editor makes the work lurid enough, throws in a little passion, he could end up with a guaranteed best-seller.

You wonder, though, how much of the present drivel does get published each year. Almost anything could go, even books described as religious books.

SUMMER THEOLOGY READING

With the dearth of old-fashioned theology books, publishers and writers have had to resort to a number of tricky titles, graphic covers, and esoteric subjects to sell "religious" books.

As each summer approaches, a number of prominent people are asked to suggest their choices for "Theological Hammock Reading," or "Theology Books for My Summer Vacation." Here could be some of their choices and comments:

Driver Louis, major league ball player: "My favorite book now is, *Is God a Blind Umpire?* by Tim Bolting. Bolting, a former shortstop, proves that any concept of God which fails to face up to the unfair salaries given to ball players by corrupt owners, is unrealistic. It shows no concern for exploitation of men by money-mad millionaires. Bolting calls all religious men to consider his

'Theology of the Diamond' as a direct challenge to resolve social inequities between players and owners."

Polly Anner, movie actress: "I have been overwhelmed by *The Love Song of Judas Iscariot* by Mamie Tishwell. This sensitive, moving novel gives us a new picture of young Judas, a man betrayed by the Roman courtesan, Rubelia. He turns to the mystic guru from Galilee for counsel and advice but is disillusioned by the crude manners of the fishermen-apostles. Judas betrays Christ to save Him from becoming like such rabble. Judas is rejoined by Rubelia and they marry, but he is killed by an angry mob of fishermen. Ms. Tishwell's portrayal of the interior growth of character in her hero is matched only by depicting the conflict in Rubelia (a part I would dearly love to play) between life at the dissolute court and her love for the sensitive Judas."

Terence O'Flay, scenic designer: "My summer reading in theology is going to be *Noah's Space Ship* by Hans Heiniken. Mr. Heiniken, a Swiss, is a former bung-maker for beer barrels, who has educated himself in archaeology, alchemy, the Bible, anthropology, and zoology. Heiniken proposes that the story of Noah's ark is a fictive device used in Genesis to tell of an invasion of earth from outer space by spacemen and their animals. He deduces that men from three lost planets, Hammon, Shemon and Japhetto (the names of Noah's sons are a cipher device), brought a new race of animals to this planet. Heiniken claims to have found lost traces of these space people in certain Alpine valleys. Swiss breakfast cereals are derived from ancient recipes of these space people. There are sketches of the space ship designed by Noah, a semi-god from the planet Arkania. Heiniken's case is plausible and cannot easily be dismissed by theology or science."

Arthur Henry-James, banker: "I have been intrigued by *The Yellow Brick Road and Mystic Paths to Self-Knowledge* by G. Wizzard. This study of the symbolic meaning of the yellow brick road in our culture is a modern version of Pilgrim's Progress, the Quest of the Grail, and rites of initiation among the Hopi Indians. Wizzard's phenomenal knowledge of the number and meanings of bricks, turns, and colors in the yellow brick road help him make present-day connections with Yoga, Zen, Tartra, and Kung Fu Paths of Enlightenment. His chapter on 'Grasshopper on the Road' is delightful. For the experienced amateur."

Roger Cream, New York gastronomical expert: "I choose as my theological book of the year, *Happy: A Gourmet Guide to Esoteric Liturgies.* This is a collaboration by Nelson Beard and Graeme Cracker. This fascinating help to self-liturgies is an absolute *must* for liturgy bugs. In addition to 14 different recipes for breads at offertory processions (the 'sour dough' recipe is a gem!), it includes a description of the winemaking process for those wanting to make their own offertory wine. There is an instant calculator to compose one's own greetings, penitential rites, meaningful kisses of peace. (Beard-Cracker claim the concept of a 'sign of peace' is not satisfied by merely flashing cards with the word 'peace.' On the other hand, the authors reject the concept of the kiss of peace as a Bacchanalian orgy.) This book is well worth its $50, but is a bit heavy for the hammock."

Henry Cramsniff, theologian: "I like *The High Priest* by Sir Roger Knack, a study of the chilling effects of a new Catholic pastor when he moves into the big city. Quietly, insidiously the priest sets out, through gossip and secret letters, to be the only priest in town, as he says, 'The High Priest.' Father O'Holey's (the hero-villain) obsession is not money, nor sex, but power. It's a kind of ecclesiastical *All About Eve,* but instead of Eve Harrington getting rid of Margo Channing, Father Mill Wrighter, a young friend of Father O'Holey, brings about the downfall of his master and he becomes 'The High Priest.' When they make this book a movie, I can see Warren Beatty in the part."

What's that? None of these books of theology are listed anywhere? No, not yet. But a share of equally silly, inane and superficial books with similar titles and themes appear regularly. What a calamity has fallen on the field of religious book publishing! Where are the Gheons, the Jorgensens, the Chestertons, the Knoxs, and all those who make religious themes matters of joy, lucidity and interest? Gone, and few are there to take their places.

Instead, we will probably be getting, in season and out, books like these.

FUTURE BOOKS

No more are there "Catholic" book lists. Some "Protestant" book publishing houses have survived and even produce a few Catholic books. Authors on Catholic subjects seek out major secular book publishers. The major religious novel in one year, so acclaimed by religious experts, was an insignificant thing called *A Nun in the Closet* by Dorothy Gilman—a slight mystery novel about a nun detective. (The late Anthony Boucher did that much better with his Sister Ursula.) Meanwhile, as has been pointed out, the secular world gave Paul Horgan's *Lamy of Santa Fe,* the biography of a bishop, a Pulitzer Prize. Scripture comes true: the children of this generation are wiser than the children of light.

Yet, given the quality of much of religious writing and thought in our day, we cannot assess blame. Books like these, alas, will be our future fare.

Theology of the Skate Board: How the Heavenly Wheels are Related to and Affected by Earthly Wheels, by Fritz Haffnagle, noted Luxembourg theologian. (Publisher: Divine Toys, Inc.)

Where Vatican II Went Wrong: By Inviting the Bishops, by Joffery Grunt, former priest, former husband, former playboy, former Catholic. (Publisher: Hangloose Press.)

Selected Curse Words as Mantras: An Exploration into the Connection between Obscenity and Meditation, by Swami Twami, President of the Cursory Cursing Society of Greasedale. (Publisher: Dirtylips and Soapwash, Inc.)

Cooking with Holy Water, by Paphnutia Anglewords, subtitled "A Catholic Culinary Compilation Consisting of Concoctions, Prayers and Horoscopes to Know What Days Are Best Astrologically for Diverse Recipes." (Published by the Kitchen Companions of St. Cuthbert's, Oddslot, Ipswich, England.)

Mars: Is It the Place Where Angels Dwell? by Willie Limepie. The author's foreword explains: "The exploration of Mars will reveal that this planet was undoubtedly the place where God's Angels dwelt and from where they came to earth on various errands. It gives a religious viewpoint and answer to *Chariot of the Gods.*" (Published by Astronauts Press, Mars.)

Adam: The First Charismatic, by John Cardinal von Donne. In this book the Cardinal from Andorra proposes that when Adam heard God's voice in the garden, it was the first speaking in tongues. The entrance of Eve onto the scene, proposes the Cardinal, created the first marriage encounter. All subsequent history, he feels, has been an attempt to get back to these starting points. (Publisher: Glossy Lalia Press.)

The Dancing Liturgy, by Otelia Leotard. In this, the author, a former ballet star, proposes that liturgy can never fully satisfy the needs of the people until it takes in the choreographic nature of mankind. An excerpt from this book, "Beginning Dance Steps for Beginning Bishops," appeared last fall in the *Guide to Episcopal Fulfillment* magazine, a quarterly published by Auxiliary Services Guide of Priest Pal, Inc., the publisher of the famous liturgy text—*The Missalino*—which produced this book.

Horizontal Meditation: An Answer to Transformation Meditation, by Dom Percy Perkins, O.S.B. In this new work, the author of the successful *Metaphysical Journeys on the Swami River* (a handbook in contemplation for fearful neophytes) has surpassed himself. The Benedictine expert in the contemplative style, points out how past meditation failed because it insisted on kneeling, on sitting, on squatting as proper bodily posture. Dom Percy of Crooked Knees, Idaho, insists that the position for meditation is stretched out horizontally, preferably on a bed. The monk envisions the monasteries of the future as vast dormitories and the contemplative as one who can manage to stay in bed all day.

We add to this: *The CB in the Pulpit,* by "Saintly Daddy" (the CB handle for Father Periwinkle Paskudnik). Father Periwinkle Paskudnik is a CB enthusiast and sees great usages for the CB in homilies and in attracting many who would not otherwise hear a sermon. Father Paskudnik believes that CB is the pulpit of tomorrow.

NORBERT GAUGHAN

If these books do not come out, as we described, others equally silly will be touted as the new "in" books and what everybody must read in order to be up to date on religion and the Church.

Oh well, at least they're reading—unless these come out as comic books.

Sometimes the confusion in the world and in religion seems like one great movie plot. Or a book outline. Or, best of all, like those mixed-up synopses for grand opera.

LOST OPERA

We are accustomed, even in the Church, to view a present crisis as the worst in history. It is *our* crisis, we are caught up in the living of it. It should be comforting then to discover a long-lost opera, which tells of a time in history when priests were undergoing identity problems much like today.

Last winter musicologists were ecstatic to learn of the discovery in a hunting lodge once owned by a Renaissance Pope, outside Rome, of the score and libretto of the opera *Il Prete con Significazione* (English scholars have called it "The Meaningful Priest"), written by the mostly unknown composer Giovanni Giuseppe Artigiano (1809-1884). Opera companies are rushing to perform this lost treasure, even though little is really known about Artigiano, who was born in the small town of San Botolfo, studied diplomacy in the Collegio de S. Ricardo in Vigornio, and went on to be acclaimed in the musical salons of Rome.

Since an outline of the plot of the opera has been published in the musical magazine *Girello* (The Whirling Turntable") we recount it here.

The hero, Giovinetto Re ("Giovinetto"—"Little John," like the German "Hans." The English name might be "Little Johnny King.") is a priest ordained five years. The opera opens on the city square of Tubingo, a university town, to which Vinetto (his nickname) has just come as the new pastor. He sings the opening aria to the villagers, "Tutti Frutti" ("You Are the Fruits of My Joy"). The townsfolk respond with the simple peasant dance, "Uovo in Birra" ("An Egg in Your Beer"), which contrasts the easy life of the priest with the hard life of the peasants. The leader of the discontented faction of the workers is Giacomo di Grappa, who sings the threatening song, "Noi Soltanto Commincia-mini" ("We've Only Just Begun." Musical note: This aria will lend itself well to weddings because of its deeper meanings.)

Vinetto is visited by some priests, his former classmates, who have taken off their clerical cassocks to don the colorful peasant garments. They invite Vinetto to do likewise, but he responds with "Clericale in Nero" ("I'd Rather Be a Cleric in Black, Than a Fool in Motley").

As Act II opens in the parish church, the taunts of Di Grappa and of his classmates have disturbed Vinetto. Alone, he ponders if his life-style as a priest is significant. Di Grappa and his followers burst in to demand he turn over his church and house to them, and they harass a few parishioners.

Enraged, Vinetto sings, "Protesta Ma Non Molesta" ("Protest But Do Not Molest"), and he drives them out, but one stays behind. It is Griselda di Grappa, daughter of the troublemaker. She tells Vinetto that she wanted to be a nun, but does not want to join the local nuns who are allied with Vinetto's priest friends in their move to get away from religious garb. Her solo, "Abiti Slegati" ("Loose Habits") in praise of religious garb, is a masterful blend of new and old elements. Vinetto, attracted to her, remembers his vows.

Act III portrays Roderico di Cane, a poet-troubador from overseas attending the annual pasta fair in the square, singing the fair's theme, "Da Minestrone al Noci" ("From Soup to Nuts"). When he meets Vinetto, Roderico describes his solution to the world's evils, "Si Abbiamo Solamento Amore" ("If We Only Have Love"). Vinetto discovers that this is what he as a priest has been lacking. Excitedly, he calls together his parish council to tell them his plan: this parish will be ruled by love. The council members listen, but disagree with him and with each other. Their song may become a classic, "The Sextet from Il Prete," as each one describes his plan while paying no attention to the other.

In Act IV in the church, Vatican officials have come to hear Vinetto's plan for a Church of Love. Vinetto describes how he will make all—priests, sisters and laity—live together and never disagree. His plan, "Il Sogno Senza Possibilita" ("The Dream Without Possibility") does not move the officials, but they offer him the title of "Monsignor." Scornfully he rejects them, "Voglio Essere Mortuo Che Rosso" ("I'd Rather Be Dead Than Red"), and they excommunicate him. Alone and dejected, he envisions himself surrounded by demons who dance around him to the strains of the exquisite "Excommunication Tarantella."

Act V, in the square, depicts Vinetto who realizes love alone cannot answer everything. He explains this to Roderico in "Amore Senza Pasta?" ("What Good Is Love Without Pasta?"). Griselda offers her love, but he sends her off to the convent to bring back the religious habit, "Un Vestito Non Fare l'Uomo, Ma e un Ajuto Fare la Femina" ("Clothes Do Not Make the Man, But Help Him Make the Woman"). The apologetic parish council want him to stay and he agrees, on a daily basis as he sings, "Un Giorno da Giorno" ("Day by Day"). A Vatican messenger annouces the excommunication has been lifted. Vinetto's book "Love in the Church" has won the "Ermie" (Erasmus) Award. Giacomo di Grappa renouces his evil ways and will enter the minor seminary at Scuolo Latina di Tre Fiuma. All join in the final song, "Dateci Shalom, Non Salume" ("Give Us 'Shalom'—Peace—and Not Salami").

This opera, deep in meaning, should reassure us that church troubles are never new. Borgia Records promises to release this work, but in view of a power struggle within the family corporation, this may take a while.

PART III

CULTURE AND THE WORD

It would appear, then, that we are more influenced by culture than we suspect. This may be the place to reflect on these aspects of life that quietly, insistently sap our energies and our strength, or on the contrary, sustain and strengthen us.

Omnipresent these days is "The News." We are all news-bugs. It surrounds us, fills up our hours and ears.

REFLECTIONS ON THE TIMES AND NEWS

The times they are a-changing, said Bob Dylan, as he opted out of them and went Nashville style.

There's no time left, for you at least, say the "Guess Who," a rock group, and we try in vain to guess, who is the you? Me?

But each bright day brings with it the promise of time's rebirth, starting off the waking hours with the possibilities of new time.

By day's end and more, in these days, it has turned out to be the same old day, one of many same days, only more so.

Because at day's end, we have heard the dismal record of that day, in what is known in the trade as the seven o'clock news.

147

It may come at 6, or 6:30, or 5:30, or even 5 o'clock, for it changes. Yet it is still the seven o'clock news.

Unless it's the eleven.

Which is the same as the seven, but more precise, which is to say, the bad news is compressed.

Why does the evening news seem more oppressing than the morning report?

Why is it harder to take, more to bear?

Is it that, by day's end, we are so weary, so frustrated, so buffetted by the small hostilities of the day that we are ready to believe the worst, or even anxious to show our worst?

But it is a fact, is it not, that it's not Cronkite nor Reasoner, not Brinkley nor Walters? It might as well be Laurel or Hardy, or Mutt and Jeff. It would be just as bad.

Could it be possible that we might, by some alchemy, move the evening news to the morning?

It might work; it could be better; it would improve the situation.

Then whatever happens afterwards, at the office, in the home or factory, or wherever, it could be easier to take.

Why would this be so? For these reasons.

Having heard that the world is almost at an end, or that wars go on, or being told of continuing evils of men to men, of young to old, or vice-versa; or after hearing of dope, dopes and dupes, of follies marital and martial, the day—no matter what happens after—becomes easier to bear.

Because all these evils would quickly be forgotten, or at least become more bearable by the process of the daily living, or loving, or plain survival.

The evening news at seven may just be too much for a full stomach, or even for an empty one.

And the news at eleven seems like too much to take to bed with you.

For which of us, no matter how strong, can bear to spend those quiet hours, or share the rest-promising moments with such anxieties, ghouls and sleep-robbing devils as are spawned by the news?

Even the talk shows, the nighttime phone conversations, the stale wit of Johnny Carson or his substitutes, can never wipe out the riots, murders and savageries of our times.

These lie upon the spirit like a badly-cooked meal upon the stomach, and come back again and again with sour and bitter taste best never experienced.

The times are really not a-changing, no matter what Bob Dylan, or weak-voiced imitations of him, tell us.

The times continue, in the seven and eleven o'clock news, to record the same facts.

They remind us of the lack of love, the growth of hate, the abundance of stupidity, the dearth of patience, the famine of concern of one human for another.

They sing a dirge, the follies of man, the follies of 1080, and 1580 and 1980, and on and on and on.

Who will deliver us from the folly of this death, said St. Paul; this kind of death, we say, this slow dying by the seven and eleven o'clock news?

Who will deliver us if not the Lord? He alone, as He best desires, in concert, in conspiracy with us, will rescue us, from ourselves, from the times, from the news.

The question thus remains: do we give meaning to our times and places? Or do they to us? The existential philosophers believe that we are what we are because of when and where we exist. It would appear the times give us our *meaning*.

MEANING

Ludwig Wittgenstein was the Viennese-born philosopher who gained fame in England's philosophical circles with Bertrand Russell and Gottlob Frege, as they introduced language analysis as a problem solver for modern philosophy. It was Russell especially who claimed to resolve some of the dilemmas in philosophy by saying that linguistic analysis would provide solutions by showing that words such as "truth," "beauty," "honor," "God," were non-meaning words.

In their book, *Wittgenstein's Vienna*, philosophers Allan Janik and Stephen Toulmin demonstrated that such was never Wittgenstein's intent. They claimed that this man's character resulted from conditions and circumstances encountered in living out his life in the special place and situation of his day. Wittgenstein, they say,

who was really an engineer, would reject what
some students of philosophy have done to him.
Teachers of philosophy have withdrawn him from
his context in the city of Vienna, out of the closing
days of the Austro-Hungarian Empire, out of that
corrupt and declining society, to consider only
Wittgenstein's writings. These are seen as cold,
abstract thoughts, independent of the life of the
man. But Janik-Toulmin show that what Vienna
and the Hapsburg Empire demanded in that day
was precisely a thorough reconstruction of every
means of expression: language, politics, art, music,
architecture. These had ceased to deliver their
basic messages, had become something else, had
failed to express the intended meanings. So instead of clarifying, which language, art, music,
etc. are supposed to do, these activities of man
added further to the chaos and confusion of that
society.

The Hapsburg monarchy is defined by the authors as "a power plagued by problems of rapid
economic change and turbulent racial minorities,
a power whose established constitutional structure was at essential points incapable of adapting
itself to the novel demands of its changing historical situation." That sends a shudder, doesn't
it? It appears so descriptive of nations today.
Vienna's leading critic then was one Karl Kraus
who hated "slovenliness in thought and expression
which is the enemy of individual integrity and
leaves one defenseless against the political decep-
tions of corrupt and hypocritical men." Kraus'

crusade instigated others to restore honesty to the social debate. Demands for honesty of communication brought about revolution in every cultural field, including Wittgenstein's philosophy.

Could this be where we are today? Our present and absolute imprecision of language allows every illiterate to say anything he wants in public places, and claim it has validity. Futhermore, he is not to be challenged. It is his right to have an "opinion." Those powerful gods, Subjectivity and Relativity, have debased words like "good," "honest," "moral," "true," "honor," "duty," and the like. The over-verbalization of our culture uses words to pour over us, surround us, drown us until it becomes a babble, devoid of meaning. On this, read George Orwell's essay "Politics and Language."

Consider the inflated language of exaggeration exemplified for example by leaders who speak in superlatives—"the greatest," "the best," "the most," whether it be an approving judgment on what the administration is doing, or a condemnation about what the critics are saying. Lies, easily recognized, are passed off in interviews by politicians, diplomats, statesmen. It is the accepted thing, the way to keep yourself loose and noncommitted, and provides convenient doors and windows for linguistic exit.

Hapsburg Vienna with its pastry-like architecture (all whipped cream and gingerbread) gave way in time to the extremes of our present buildings. These are great for business, efficiency, standardization. They are absolutely ruinous for the human spirit—windowless, natural lightless, cold, functional warrens and hutches in which human animals can scurry to and fro without ever having a genuine human experience. The barrenness of modern art is all too evident. Its philosophy is exemplified by the passed-along statement which offends nobody: "It means whatever you want it to mean." Pop Art was one great big, but expensive, joke. Some art is a betrayal of its ancient handmaiden, aesthetics. Popular music has sunk to its present nadir, as we plumb the depths of noise by bursting barriers of sound and shrillness. Modern serious music flirts with technology and electronics. That pure clear music once thought to be part of God's own creation, and heard in the music of the planets, can no longer even be heard by our besieged ears.

Literature is the non-book with no coherence, little thought and paucity of language, or it is a dull, repetitious, boring retelling of erotica or meaninglessness. McLuhan tried to tell us a few years ago that the medium is the message. Then the message of the media today is that there is no more message. It is no longer a case that we cannot hear the tune. We have even forgotten the chords. We cannot vamp. We have forgotten the melody.

In affairs of religion this abuse of language has robbed us of opportunities to discover basic meanings. We took away religious symbols because we said they no longer communicate. We trotted out the manufactured symbols which communicate even less, or convey only sterility, barrenness, alienation. Partisans on all sides of religious battles pile up words like dead bodies to muffle the sounds of their enemies. Scripture, the writings of Church Fathers, the sayings of popes, are plundered and pillaged, yanked out of context, twisted and bent, to make them mean things never intended by God or man.

It is not that we have built a Tower of Babel. Then there was at least a tower. Man, who glories in the fact that he is lower than the angels and rejoiced that he could share meaning with others, no longer means anything to anyone, even to himself.

What will rescue us from this empty, meaningless meaning? Possibly discipline, precision, candor, honesty, hard work. Above all, we need to tell truth to one another—in charity, of course. We must believe our first truth is the meaning we make or find in our individual selves.

So not from the times, not from the place, but from what we are: God's sons and daughters.

That takes some doing. All about us, the skepticism, boredom and emptiness of life are preached, even sung. Pope Paul VI himself has commented on the pessimism of the literature of our time: "Perhaps never before, as much as in our day, have literature, the theater, art and philosophical thought borne more merciless witness to man's deficiency, his mental debility, his domination by sensuality, his moral hypocrisy, his facile delinquency, his increasing cruelty, his possible abasement, his inconsistent personality. All complacent accusations are based on a terrible and seemingly irrefutable argument: Such is man, such is the great and miserable son of this century. This is the true reality of life [December 20, 1968]."

Very possibly the theme song of our days may well be the song made popular by Peggy Lee.

IS THAT ALL THERE IS?

"Is That All There Is?" hangs about as a "standard" and is one that receives many requests to be played. The song has an interesting melodic line, but the lyrics are particularly curious. It purports to be the lament of a woman who has seen one after another of life's highpoints wiped away or dissolved into nothing. After each such letdown, the singer suggests that if that's all there is, life is a fraud and perhaps someone should break out the booze. The lady will not even agree to suicide as a way out of the fraud, because even the afterlife may turn out to be mere disillusionment.

Perhaps the popularity of the song lies in the fact that it echoed the bored, jaded, world-weary mood of the day. It could be a song of the middle class, affluent society, of Americans who have seen everything, tasted everything, experienced everything and found that all these turn into ashes. The song could in a way be a condemnation of our culture, which has succeeded in painting everything a dull, insipid gray color of pure blah.

The ancient Greek and Roman philosophers talked about the "golden mean" (the aurea mediocritas"). It was a way of life, a vehicle by which a man could live calmly and peaceably without getting torn apart, pulled by opposite passions. All he had to do was to choose the middle road. But the middle road was "mediocritas"—mediocrity, today an unpleasant word which we reject in theory while espousing it in fact. The ancients proposed that while you lived this way, you had to be aware of the other dimensions, even if you chose deliberately to walk a middle course. Moderns do not accept that. We have translated that into meaning: don't learn anything new, or try new roads. We must not break out of the boundaries of our middle class life in any way. We are safer not to challenge its assumptions and to remain closed to new, but dangerous, possibilities. Not the middle road as if knowing both extremes; but the same road, unaware of anything else.

In that sense many of our leaders are mediocre in the pejorative sense. The art we call popular is mediocre, as is most music, writing, or culture. As one author observed, we have moved from the time of the Renaissance where everything meant everything, to our present enlightened state where nothing means anything.

Perhaps we do not have more challenging leaders because we do not deserve them at this time. The ones which the Lord gave us in past years we quickly digested and regurgitated to create rather a popular, easy-answer leadership of simple values, which demanded little of us. Those who want to stick their head above the crowd either find out quickly that it doesn't pay and they are pushed back into the common mediocrity, or we quickly surround them with such instant adulation, wealth and fame that they dare not be what they set out to be, and settle back to become "popular" leaders, which is to say, leaders of mediocrity.

Is that all there is? Not if you accept the Gospel. Not if you believe that the Christian challenge is to new life and new possibilities. Not if you believe in a new world a-coming, a Kingdom of God on its way, a humanity growing and enlarged to achieve even greater accomplishments in the name of God. This does mean breaking through mediocrity, being willing to become individual, different, unusual. If one is not prepared for that, then one is doomed to mediocrity.

Schopenhauer says somewhere that there are only two choices for man—boredom or suffering. We don't want to suffer. So we are condemned to be bored.

Meanwhile, as boredom sets in we try to whip ourselves into a pale imitation of life and activity by increasing our social calendar, by accepting more things to do and places to go. We are so anxious to prove that there is more to life than just a round of meals and the monotony of daily life, that we seek stimulation in television interviews and conversations, the phone shows, talk shows and the latest TV movie. All these quickly turn to be dull, tired, stale repetitions, which leave us even emptier and more bored. After you have condemned everything and everyone, after you have torn everything down, after you have agreed that no one is doing anything about the situation, what's left? You can only exist by turning off the challenge of living life according to the Gospel. You alibi by pretending that "that's the way it is," and "there's nothing you can do about it." If that's all there is, we better break out the booze. Or drugs. Or just stagnate quietly as the world ends, not with the bang, but quietly flickers out—not even with a whimper.

With such a view, no wonder we all feel let down, bruised, or just plain unwell. The current view may be true: the world's one great big hospital and all of us are patients in it.

THERAPY

Is the world a hospital? Reading, viewing TV, hearing radio, you would certainly think so. Words like "sick," "unhealthy," "disturbed," "odd," "strange," are tossed around indiscriminately about people as if the descriptions and applications were natural. "Therapy" has become "in." It is being advised as necessary for practically everyone as a natural corrective for being alive. It's no longer a great big beautiful world; it's a sick world filled with sick people, a gigantic hospital in which no one is well, especially the administration and staff.

Those thoughts arose from a reading of "Meditations" by the pseudonymous author, Aristides, in

The American Scholar (Spring 1976). Everything
has become a problem to be considered, said the
writer. There is little talk anymore about the joy of
life, of growing up, of maturing. We all have to
learn how to cope. See what we are faced with.
There is the problem of children, the problem of
age, the problems of marriage, the problem of
youth, the problem of nutrition. Name it: it's a
problem. So many problems eventually become a
problem in themselves, says "Aristides," that is,
the problem of problems.

Why this preoccupation with problems? Why
such a negativism? When "Aristides" ponders as
to why this might be, he thinks it may be due to the
gospel according to St. Freud. In fact, one of
Freud's interpreters, Philip Rieff, wrote a book
The Triumph of the Therapeutic. Therapy has tri-
umphed. "Therapeutic" is the view that "what is
more significant in life is played out in one's
mind." Not in reality, not in the real world, but the
reality as revealed in one's self. Life is a drama;
life is conflict; life is tension; life is confronting
one's self. This sets up battles: not reality, but
what we "feel" about it. In this immense and intense soul-searching, much of our culture has
come up with one attitude: grievance, anxiety. All
of which, however, can only be solved by therapy.
Therapy is life. What is human is sick; what is
human needs therapy. Recreation is therapy.
Reading is therapy. Sex is therapy. Religion is
therapy. If you're alive you need therapy.

The *New York Times Magazine* carried an article about the "new priests," psychiatrists. The author labeled one branch of psychiatrists as "Catholic," another "Protestant." The names had nothing to do with religion. They applied to attitudes or viewpoints of the "healing" approaches. The point was well made, however. Since the rise of the doctrines of Freud (Europeans are amazed at the way Americans have canonized Freud. Americans who deny infallibility to the Pope readily bestow it on the Viennese doctor), life is pathology. Everybody knows what a "Freudian slip" is. Each person looks for such slips of behavior by which his neighbor will betray an inner sickness. Pessimism breeds upon itself. Scarce is that TV program when the person who is normal, by program's end does not reveal a sickness crying out for therapy. Almost all soap opera characters appear to be fugitives from sanity. Possibly this explains why the movie, *One Flew Over the Cuckoo's Nest,* was chosen for an Academy Award; it illustrated therapy. The sickies in the theater laughed at the sicker ones inside the institution; both laugh at staff and administration who proved to be the sickest of all.

As hinted above, therapy has even crept into the field of religion. Dr. Louis Dupre, a Belgian Catholic philosopher of religion, wrote in *The Christian Century* (4/7/76) about "The Wounded Self: The Religious Meaning of Mental Suffering." In his view, those who are mentally sick are representatives of the alienation of all humanity. All humanity is alienated. True, but alienation is

CULTURE AND THE WORD

not sickness as such. It is a fashionable word but what it means theologically is not the same medically.

But in our preoccupation with therapy, religion for some is only therapy. Religion can be therapy; it is never merely that, nor always that. Otherwise we believe that God, the good Creator, has made all men defective; God the merciful has given no man normalcy. Do we really believe it is normal that man is born ill, that all those born of women need therapy?

Christian theology invoked the concept of original sin to account for a flaw in human nature; yet this was by no means a disease. We called upon the doctrine of grace to help man rise above the effects of sin. But if all men are sick from birth, and if religion is only therapy, down go concepts of faith, and love, and God's mercy.

Unfortunately, the idea of religion as therapy is a mainstay of our culture. There are persons who suspect that they and all others are "religiously" sick. Some young men and women take on the religious life because they perceive themselves in need, and find such religious careers as a means of therapy. They use ways to help others whom they perceive to need treatment. But religious vocation and life are not and never were meant to be therapeutic. This may be why many left that life. It did not treat their ills.

"Aristides" is right. There is will; there is imagination; and may we add, there is God's grace and God's love. These keep men balanced. If we are

161

not to conceive of life as a permanent sickness from which we recover only by death, the truth may be in the question and answer of the old Baltimore Catechism: Why did God make us? To know Him, to love Him, to serve Him, to be happy with Him *in this world*—and in the next.

But is our need for "therapy" the result of the over-emphasis now on feeling, emotion? This began as a necessary corrective to our undue stress on reason alone. But then we counted only feeling and emotion as valuable; so reasoning began to decline as a healthy and necessary activity of man.

SOUND REASON

In a diocese far away and not so long ago, the celebrant priest and the nuns in a convent had agreed upon a special liturgy to open a day-long workshop. It also had been agreed that the second reading of the Mass would be St. Paul's Hymn to Charity, 1 Corinthians, chapter 13. When the celebrant showed up for the Mass, he was approached by one sister who had a special request. In his kindness would he allow that the sister who would do this reading to substitute for the word "charity," wherever it occurred, the word "woman." Thus it would read: "Woman is patient, is kind, never perverse or proud." Apart from certain interesting angles, e.g., "faith, hope and woman persist," or "if I lack woman I am no better than the clash of cymbals," the request was turned down by the priest, who was probably (of this there is no knowledge) labeled a male chauvinist you-know-what, or an outdated ecclesiastic.

Consider another item. A priest visiting a university town in America noted the following. A student group runs its own pornographic cinema on campus and charges a good price. But the profits made from this enterprise are used to finance a program of help for rape victims.

Both priests merely mentioned their stories in passing. They are told here as examples showing the breakdown of sound thinking among the so-called educated groups. Today, sentimentality, piety and banality are substitutes for rational thinking, which is considered cold, dogmatic, and unchristian. In the first story, the nun obviously did not understand the meaning of scripture as "the inspired Word of God." She had not pondered the implications of making her words, even for a good cause, replace the phrases chosen by the Holy Spirit. In the second story, the "well-intentioned" (?) promoters obviously failed to see any connecting link between those who patronize their movies and the victims of sexual assault.

Sound thinking is dead. Presently seminarians are being ordained who have not had a single formal course in philosophy. It is said that philosophy is no longer needed for the priest; a good heart suffices. Curriculum experts in the seminary have beefed up courses on Sacred Scripture and placed their bets on "involvement" and field internship instead of sound learning. Educators of priests have missed the point that the priest as a rational being must know the tools of thinking, the disciplines of the intellect, and the cold, hard but necessary facts of logic. This, even before he can preach, teach, be a leader.

In 1970 a proposed program of priestly formation had added philosophy as a necessary subject for the future priest. The Congregation for Catholic Education under Cardinal Garrone later reiterated the same idea. Archbishop Jadot, as he spoke to the bishops in November of 1974, recommended this basic need. What was it? That the equivalent of two years' study be spent in Christian philosophy by seminarians. This would amount to six courses or eighteen credits. Despite these pleas, the call to train in sound thinking is still far from being implemented. Why? Because there yet exists a hostility to philosophy. We are in the era of scripture studies, and the "soft sciences"; unfortunately these alone are being taught as "pastoral," needing no philosophy. We are in the era of a moral theology proposed without basic principles, which says that "all you need is love to do the right thing." Philosophy once was considered important because it taught us to make right distinctions, to be precise, to be consistent, to be logical. Maritain said: man's glory is that only man can make a distinction. Yet philosophy has now been deemed unnecessary. Catholic leadership still embraces the old Martin Luther doctrine that reason is the tool of the devil and hostile to faith. We decry the breakdown of sound sermons, the confusing statements of some people in the Church which border close to the irrational. We never think that this might be because they have not learned the principles of reasoning.

But there is no body of teaching in the Church, not even scripture, which is not guided by the necessity to understand, to define, to be precise, to learn the deeper implications and to explicate the corollaries. In teaching young people today one always encounters among freshmen, up to seniors, the statement, "that, after all, is only your opinion." The American college student has not understood that there are necessary truths (not merely about religion) and that the possibility of achieving truth exists. No wonder that attempts to discuss doctrines, ideas, actions and teachings, with sound reasoning, break up because one party, unschooled in philosophy, ends up by claiming, "it's only a matter of semantics," "that's just your opinion," "that's not the way I feel," etc.

St. Paul said the Christian must always be able to give an account of his faith. This injunction applies all the more to the priest as preacher and teacher, and to the religious leader. We are so caught up in the relativism of the day which is somehow mixed up with our view of the concept of democracy, that we are told we can never say that any person is, in fact, wrong.

It was bad enough to have lost the teaching of Latin and its formal discipline which gave the learner the joy of language used well and precisely. It is appalling that modern opinion-makers in the Church have no grasp of the fundamental and logical tenets of their English language. One is almost tempted to grieve with Professor Higgins when he heard the distorted noises come from Eliza which passed as the English language. It is ridiculous that when you ask a person to be precise, to define, to make distinctions, you are accused of being uncharitable. But that's where we are today. Until the responsible ones get their personnel, the future leaders, back to basic philosophy, we shall have to continue in this Babel-like situation.

COLLAGE

Little wonder that a speaker described some of the present thinking and teaching in the field of religion as "collage thinking." It was an apt metaphor. In fact the word fits the thought of the age. This is a time not when art imitates nature, but nature imitates art. Collage art became popular in the early 20s. Today collage is less visible in the art field, still performed, but now done by the masses. Every craft and art store has kits and materials for collage and decoupage (a technique which is similar to collage).

Collage, in a non-technical sense, is the procedure by which bits and snippets of things are placed together, not quite randomly, against a background and within a space that allows these fragments of many things to give the illusion and appearance of unity. Non-related things are so arranged that they look as one. *Decoupage* is transferring a picture from its original source to another place and to another object. The original, in a fashion, is removed from where it belongs and placed elsewhere as if it belonged there: on lampshades, trays, boxes, and the like. It's not where it was originally meant to be, nor indeed what it was.

Perhaps you can see now why the metaphor of "collage thinking" is apt. In such activity there appears to be little continuity, unity, relatedness in the things discussed, written or taught. This occurs in many fields. A *New York Times'* American History test revealed an abysmal knowledge of American history on the part of college freshmen. These students did not even have the most elementary facts. Those who analyzed the results noticed the trend away from factual content to "concepts" —and some teachers were not giving even those.

"Collage" can apply to some of the kinds of thinking and teaching in religion too. People are given snippets of things, bits and pieces from a variety of sources, none of which really cohere, but are claimed to be "one faith." Ideas and concepts are cut out of other fabrics and disciplines and suddenly transferred to the fields of doctrine, morals, faith, in the style of decoupage, as if they belonged there automatically.

Let's give examples. The young Catholic student is exposed in some Christian Doctrine experiences to the multiple fads that have been substituted for teaching doctrine. He is given a bit of behavioral science, a little attitude formation, much con-

167

sciousness-raising, bits and pieces of scripture, pop contemporary problems, and all of it is lumped under the title of "Christian Doctrine." This is not to blame the teachers. Nor indeed the administrators and planners of "production." Rather, the mixed bag of thinking (if it be that) stems from the lack of cohesion at upper levels: the manipulators of CCD materials for sale, the promoters of books and printed pieces by "experts" as service aids. Or—the hustle for the buck.

At the higher levels, college courses in religion have suffered from this lack of cohesion. The student flits from one pop course to the other, always thinking, and sometimes being told, that they relate, are all interconnected, are of one cloth. Yet they rarely are. Collage thinking flows over to priestly preaching and teaching where the Sunday sermon is a melange of pop psychology, sociological reviews of the week's news, and personal opinions—opinions, not facts, not even "truths."

Collage as an art form is not as popular today. It takes discipline and skill to create a unity, any unity; the unity of form in a painting or drawing. Collage was born shortly after Dada and the aberrations of the New Art which flowed from a society which had lost its belief in the oneness of things. It was a time, much like now, when all concentration was rather on the confusion, the random, the happenstance.

Fifty years later, collage has moved into thought. Now it particularly blossoms in religious and philosophical thinking in the new (i.e., offbeat) excursions into techniques in spirituality, and into some classy manipulation of scripture texts under categories that just do not apply.

The "decoupage" metaphor comes true in the attempt to translate awareness technique, group dynamics, and Eastern religions (badly assimilated) into the framework of Christianity. This is not to say that such things might not be done or should not be done. Rather the assertion made here is that it is too often done badly, in amateur fashion, forced into the constricts of Christian truth to change them, rather than to be assimilated. In older times the result was called "syncretism." That was an abomination to the Fathers of the Church. Whether syncretism or collage, the practice debases thought and teaching about religion and especially the Christian faith. It deludes; it passes off many variegated and unrelated things as one truth, one word, one faith, one baptism. But they are not.

Reason was closely related to understanding. In Saroyan's *The Time of Your Life,* one character kept saying, "There's no foundation all the way down the line." Yes, no foundation—better still, little or no understanding. That may be where we are.

NO UNDERSTANDING

In a course taught at a Catholic college, a basic introduction to the catechism, elevated with the title "Introduction to Theology," a friend received these answers in the examination. Asked to name three angels in scripture, one student supplied, "the Father, the Son and the Holy Spirit." A definition of "Paraclete" was: "Someone who is a nonbeliever." To explain "Creed," a student offered this: "national origin." For "Sacrament" the definition given was: "A sin against the Church."

There were many such blunders. The teacher was not unduly disturbed at this. These Catholic students somewhere received a preliminary introduction to Catholicity in a Catholic school, CCD courses, or through Sunday sermons. The results were not the fault of CCD directors or teachers. It was best put by Stephen Harrigan in the *Atlantic* (January 1977), writing on "St. Patrick's and the Prospect of Hell." Going back to a post-Vatican II Catholic school, comparing it to his "hell-fire and damnation" courses, Harrigan says, ". . . postconciliar Catholicism seemed to me essentially a social skill . . . ."

The 1978 Synod was about "Catechetics" and that may have been good. If one aspect of Catholic teaching is ignored, treated lightly, not funded enough, or at the mercy of drifting currents, it is catechetics. Once more, no blame is attributed to the present teachers and directors. They are serious, well-intentioned, high-minded persons. They have, however, been caught up in the educational syndrome of the day.

To explain, at Vatican II's end it was said, and rightly, too much catechism was memory work. The students memorized the answers but understood them poorly. Today students understand what they are saying, but the difficulty is they do not understand *why* it is so. If that sounds paradoxical, an example may help. The Catholic student is bright, sharp, good-hearted and caught up in the social apostolate. These young people spend free time to help in hospitals, take care of the elderly, visit the sick. But the young do not understand why they are doing it. They may as well be included in the category of "the good pagan." Even the pagan does these things, says Our Lord, adding that what is required is faith and prayer. It is this understanding of the need for faith and prayer that is particularly lacking. Students know all the right words, but understand only dimly the meaning and application of the words they say. At a confirmation ceremony a child will tell you now that the sacrament of confirmation will help him become "a mature Christian." The only problem is, he doesn't know what a Christian is, and he does not understand what the implications of maturity are. And he has not yet learned that to be a Catholic is to believe certain things which make his values different from those of the world about him.

We have had an explosion of knowledge all the way down the line, thanks to the modern communication techniques. Yet there has been no commensurate growth of understanding of what the Catholic Church teaches or means to me personally.

One bishop discussed pastoral planning and admitted that the hardest problem he and his priests faced in his diocese was to decide exactly what it meant to be a Catholic today. What doctrines were to be held? What doctrines were to be taught and shared? It was not just liturgical change which had brought anger and confusion to Catholics. Once some things changed, it appeared that everything was open to change. It betrayed a lack of understanding of the doctrine of the Church when some people at Detroit asked the American bishops to repeal the "law" (not doctrine) of the indissolubility of marriage. If we changed fish on Friday and allowed nuns and priests to leave, why not change this teaching? Well, we say, people do not know the difference between discipline and doctrine. Yes, except we made discipline as strong as doctrine, and once we weakened discipline and tampered with some doctrine (such as Purgatory, indulgences, scripture interpretations), then anything could be understood in the new way. It appeared to many in and outside the Church that we were in an age when any doctrine was up for change. Rather than accept some "false" teachings, we tolerated schism and separation. Today we call these "far right" or "far left" opinions about Catholic doctrine. But can anybody now be held responsible?

NO UNDERSTANDING

This is not to lament, but to report about the present condition of teaching Catholic doctrine. The situation is not new. In times of social change and confusion, new or old errors keep appearing. We are consistent with the mood of the day where we were told we must change in order to keep up to date. Now we believe that everything must change in order to keep up to date. Is the end in view? Will the Synod bring stability in catechetics? Hardly. Will the *National Catholic Directory* establish the lines beyond which a person is no longer holding Catholic teaching? That's doubtful. In the 40s a book appeared, *France Pagan,* in which it was claimed the eldest daughter of the Church had to be rechristianized. Does our evangelization begin with the unchurched, who hold no beliefs? Or do we begin within our own Church to reach that great segment of people who hold mixed, confused, or no beliefs, but still count themselves Catholic because it is convenient? If some say we must be "pastoral" and allow all of these contradictions to exist side-by-side, so be it. However, if we hold that a confession of faith, a creed, a statement of basic doctrine every Sunday states what Catholics believe and must believe, then we had better begin again to teach just that.

Yet along with the appeal to emotions, the distrust of reason, the failure to understand, arises a new development: the lack of civility.

CIVILITY

"City" has become "inner city." Country has become "suburbs" (beyond the city), potential land for development. Country folk are still different from city folk. Country people ("rudes" in Latin) became the original of "rude"; city people gave us "civility" ("cives" from "civitas," the Latin word for city).

A book, *The Country and the City*, by Raymond Williams, gathered together much of the writing over the ages contrasting the two: city and country. The volume was no paean to country living. Neither was it a condemnation of the city as the source of sin and discontent, as scripture and religious writings sometimes hint. The book did restate something that we often forget—city people who went off to live on country estates could only do so because they had available cheap, or slave labor. It was the lower class, not gentle-folk, who tilled the land, did the laundry, cooked the meals, did the cleaning, and allowed the city people to live "civilly" in the country.

Futhermore, it needs to be remembered that from pre-Roman times only to the late 19th century, "the people" usually meant the articulate, educated, well-bred, "civil" people, as contrasted to the unknown, unseen, behind-the-scenes mob, rabble, riff-raff, lower classes. Even "Mr." "Signor," "Messer," "Herr" were titles for "respectable" people, people of "moment" and worth. Only in recent history have such designations become applicable to all lower classes, or at least since the French Revolution.

The subject was addressed by Ferdinand Mount in "The Recovery of Civility" (*Encounter*, July 1973). He took for granted that it is common knowledge that "civility" has been on the wane. He cited the Spanish philosopher Ortega y Gasset, who believed that "restrictions, standards, courtesy, indirect methods, justice, reason" stem from a "radical, progressive desire on the part of each individual to take others into consideration," and is based on, "the will to live in common." That is "civility." Barbarism, says the philosopher, "is the tendency to dissociation."

Examples of loss of civility are common. Here are some assumptions made by some supposedly literate young people at colleges and universities: shout down opponents, take over buildings, chant obscenities, and harass those who disagree. No less uncivil, however, are some of the techniques of past and present White House occupants in treating those who disagree as "enemies," who seek to exacerbate them by legal, or illegal, techniques.

Add to this the "guerilla" movement spirit, seeking to punish all who are civil servants of the regime, as well as the civilians caught up in the conflict.

Nor are these losses of civility only in political or academic life. Incivility has crept even into some ecclesial matters, with loss of restraint, respect for persons and individuals, and even name-calling (not limited to one side or another) substituting for reasoned discourse.

What seems to have happened is that the need for self-development and moral character of ruler and ruled has generally been forgotten. Civility was based on Greek and Stoic philosophy, and particularly the "natural law" concepts of Seneca, the pagan philosopher. Christian teaching added more: civility, reverence, piety (respect) were based on God's fatherhood and our common brotherhood in Christ. Yet, Christians forget this.

President Nixon, who called for civility at the end of the Vietnam War—"Let us once again learn to debate our differences with civility and decency"—did great harm to civility through the machinations of his appointees. Nixon's advisers exceeded Plato and Machiavelli, who said the ruler can deceive the people because he has greater responsibility and thus is excused from the restraints for lesser men. (Succeeding administrations have not learned differently.)

Such positions were rejected by Christian thought, which held lies and deceit in loathing. The Fathers invoked even Cicero, "that reason requires nothing be done by treason, by dissimulation, by deceit."

The disregard for civility by some "well-intentioned" today stems from a passion for what they conceive of justice, the delays of modern society in achieving that justice, eradication of poverty, and making a better world.

But one abuse is never to be used to correct another, no matter in however worthy a cause. Lack of civility is an abuse. The invasions of privacy by teachers in schools, social workers in the state, teachers in the Church's institutions, all seek to bring about attitudinal changes in the children by deriding the "old fogey," "Archie Bunker," "racist" attitudes of the parents.

Perhaps the first necessary attitudinal change is in our concept of civility itself. We need a return to respect, consideration for others and their differences. We need the belief of Ortega y Gasset as he wrote "A man is uncivilised, barbarian in the degree in which he does not take others into account." By that standard, our age, which prides itself as being at the peak of the progress of civilization, may be the must uncivilized of all.

This delicate fabric of society, this role in our social order, has been examined by some sociologists. In civility, in the social order, there is a code, an unwritten pattern of behavior that helps us get through our days. The best observer of this phenomenon is Erving Goffman.

SIGNALS

Erving Goffman has been known in the past mostly by psychologists, social work students, and sociologists. But his recent books, especially *Relations in Public,* received front page treatment in the *New York Times Book Review.* All his books deserve reading by anyone interested in the things that happen when people interact in society. One earlier study, *Interaction Ritual,* is a good example of interesting insights which can shed light on the insecurities of religious people (priests, nuns) in society.

Goffman, who taught sociology at Berkeley, is concerned with what we really say by our casual phrases, glances, civilities whenever we meet others. Everyone is bound, he sees, by rules of conduct of two kinds: obligations—how a person is morally constrained to conduct himself; and expectations—how others are morally bound to act toward him. These rules are constraints—i.e., we and others are to act in a particular way. These constraints can be pleasant, or unpleasant. Because we *expect* others to follow rules of conduct, we commit ourselves to particular images of ourself; that is, we must act like persons who can be expected to follow particular rules. Because a person treats others in a particular way, and is to be treated by them in a special way, he must make certain that it will be possible for him to act and to be this kind of person.

When rules of conduct are broken, unexpected things happen, to the one with the obligation who should have governed himself by the rule, and to the other with the expectation who is threatened now by this change of behavior.

For, Goffman sees, such rules of conduct are a way of communication, by which we confirm ourselves, our special selves, our view of self. Some are ceremonial rules—ways which guide conduct in secondary significance, where special signals are sent, which become etiquette, codes of specialized behavior, and are made up of two components: deference and demeanor.

Deference means, according to Goffman, appreciation given to a recipient, marks of devotion, or "status" rituals. (Thus, "Father," "Sister" are such deferential terms which are given to persons in socio-religious settings.) Deference implies "regard," which may be real or feigned, and may not be what is "personally" thought of a person. But deference is given because he is a representative of something (i.e., a priest represents God, the Church, religion). Deference implies reciprocal obligations; the recipient must respond, acknowledge, say something. He must maintain the role, the ceremonial image of self. Deference also can imply "avoidance" rituals, things not to be done— i.e., you must never call Father and Sister by the first name without the title. For Father to insist that you call him by a first name, however, is to destroy deference, which sends out a confusing set of signals to the other person.

Which brings us to "demeanor." This involves ceremonial behavior conveyed through deportment, dress, bearing, which express that the person is of certain desirable (or undesirable) qualities. Good demeanor displays sincerity, devotion, self-control, appreciation of certain values. (We used to hear of "priestly demeanor" or "deportment," which said the priest was a certain kind of man and could be safely approached for certain services.) Well-demeanored behavior promotes deference. But deference demands that the person to whom it is given conduct himself with good demeanor, returning his deference to those present.

Goffman's ideas set up many questions. Older priests are unhappy because the title "Father" is no longer given with deference, because of the confusion since "Father" no longer identifies a certain kind of person. A young "Sister" is unhappy because the title is an affront to her individual personhood, and demands she react in a way that may not be her real self. The religious garb question is another facet of the problem. The garb elicited ceremonial reactions, but some modern nuns wanted more personalized reactions based on self. Refusal to wear the special clothes, while remaining in the role, to get a personal response rather than a ceremonial response may be praiseworthy, but it runs the risk of confusing signals to others who interact. Wearing modern garb sends out another set of signals, since it becomes another kind of "uniform" of the conformed secular society. Hostility results on both sides because of the unfamiliar, and not knowing how to react.

Perhaps, as Goffman seems to lead one to wonder, how much of any interaction is truly personal? To how many—even ourselves—do we reveal or communicate our special selves? It's interesting, or as the King of Siam said, "It's a puzzlement!"

The social fabric has some rules: unwritten or written. But as the late Stewart Alsop once wrote (speaking of the Pentagon Papers as stolen property, accepted and used by *The New York Times*), "nobody plays by the rules anymore." The concept of "civil disobedience"—"breaking the laws in which the law breaker does not believe," as Alsop defined it—is an accepted social technique. What this does in fact is to create a mood, a spirit, that any law (read: rule, regulation, rubric, by-law, etc.) can be ignored at any time by the one who feels it does not apply to him, or because it hinders or retards him from the goals he seeks.

RULES

Admittedly, it is easy to generalize here and so make errors of judgment. Not all laws, rules, regulations, rubrics are of the same import; not all have the same value; not all have the same implications. (Remember when the catechism used to talk about parvity of matter in venial sins?) But once the mood is created, that any rule can be broken at will with impunity, then you open everything to the possibility of subjective interpretation and individual choice. Even worse, there arises the possibility of what the philosophers of old called "solipsism"—namely, moving, living, and existing in a world all to yourself, and with no bridge to another's world.

This "no rules for me" religion has as its symbol, "autonomy." Michael Novak in an early book, *Ascent of the Mountain, Flight of the Dove,* called it the foundation stone of the new "invisible and unorganized religion." Unorganized religion can be anybody's, without any rules and regulations. No other man can make demands on it, except as you will. But to operate this one-man religion, it becomes necessary for the individual to "sell his religion to others," to take it into the marketplace, in order to do something together. But in every case it is doomed to failure because there must be no pattern, no rules, no regulations. There is no body, no authority, no institution which has the right to make them!

This is precisely the turmoil resulting from fulmination past and present against "organized religion." The "institution" is the enemy because it imposes rules and threatens autonomy. Of course, you can "play the rules of the game" of the institution, but you do this only to be able to do your own thing within one "framework." When the game is no longer worth it, you stop playing and get out.

We forget that Christianity is a "rules" religion. The early professions of faith, or creeds, laid down rules—"If anyone wants to profess the Catholic Faith, this he must believe," etc. That very St. Paul who is quoted as saying, "We are free with the freedom of the sons of God," acted and presumed as if he had the right to make rules which others should have the willingness to obey. That same St. John who is quoted so much about the primacy of love and telling us that God is love, still wrote in his Gospel and in the letters as if there were rules to be followed in accepting Jesus. That is why John is so hard on the leaders of the people; they had their own rules and would not submit to the rules which stemmed from accepting Jesus as Lord. Throughout the history of the Church, in meetings of Christians in synods, councils, provinces, they acted as if the Christian faith obligated them to set up lines within which Christians could operate, and outside of which a Christian could no longer honestly be called a Christian. Gradually, too many minor rules were held as if they were major. A profusion of rules without meaning behind them, led to a sterile pattern of mindless conformity demanded by some. Sadly, religion came to be thought of as mere rules.

Now we may be at the other extreme. The invisible religion has no rules, except to set up the authority of the individual, with autonomy as the sole arbiter. But here's the catch. That same individual sets up his own rules as the rules by which others must regulate their religion as it affects him! This is the outcome of one aspect of this "new freedom." Priests who rail against rules from Rome, Washington, or local bishops, set up the most absurd and strictest kind of rules for their people. ("You *must not* take Communion in the hand," "You *must* sing this folk song," "You *must* enjoy this experience.") The very avant-garde who want a wedding ceremony where they make the rules are imposing their vision as the rules for the guests who come. The various associations which have set themselves up as havens of freedom from a rule-oriented Church soon find themselves wrangling by rules, about rules, as to how far they want to go without rules. It is a vicious and unending process and we are enmeshed by it.

Two childhood games come to mind. The first is "The King of the Hill"—you remember, where a child is on the top of the mound and others try to dislodge him and take his place. They in turn are to be dislodged. Another game is the one where a line is drawn, and you dare someone to cross it. Well, they cross it, of course, and the drawn line keeps moving backwards until there is no line. Does that describe some aspects of the present situation? Until the lines are redrawn and we accept some rules as part of a Christian willingness to define membership in the Body of Christ, we just may continue to have the present disarray. Meanwhile, who's this week's "King of the Hill?"

Since politics is a by-product of the social order, if a society is ruleless, can its politics be far behind? This ruleless society is well seen in microcosm in that one ever-growing facet of modern life, politics.

POLITICS AND THE LIE

It was at the time that Father Robert Drinan was running for office, with then Father McLaughlin trying for a political post in Connecticut, that the article appeared in the *New York Review of Books*. The late Hannah Arendt, the prestigious philosopher with a remarkably keen intellect, was discussing a question which had engaged her often before: "Truth in Politics," and "Lying in Politics." The questions raised by Miss Arendt made you ask, how could a priest survive in the political arena? Would he not have to lie? Would he not be forced to dissemble? What would a priest, brought up on the doctrine of the Fathers of the Church that it was wrong to tell even a small lie, do when faced with the pressures to hide secret deals? Would he distort the truth, or disclaim kinds of knowledge which he in fact had?

Hannah Arendt could stir up such questions. This keen Jewish woman who wrote her doctoral thesis on "St. Augustine and the Love of God," who paid great tribute to Pope John XXIII in her article, "A Christian on St. Peter's Chair from 1958 to 1963," was a person who could speak of Thomas Aquinas, Augustine, the Fathers of the Church, and modern philosophers in a pellucid fashion.

It is this whole question of lying in public, by public figures (not just by politicians, nor just by priests) that attacks the heart of our land. This effect has been brought about, as Hannah Arendt said, partly by the new public relations managers in government. They have been trained in Madison Avenue advertising to know that people can be manipulated to "buy" opinions and political views. To quote Miss Arendt, "the psychological premise of human manipulability has become one of the chief wares that is sold on the market of common and learned opinion." Which brings us to this point: the tendency today to turn everything into a political issue, even religion. This, along with the lie, has resulted in destruction of public trust in the social fabric.

Max Weber, a founding father of sociology, spoke of "Politics as a Vocation." He understood politics to mean "the influencing of the leadership." When he discusses the relation of ethics and politics, Weber reports that in numerous cases the attainment of "good" ends is bound to the fact that one must be willing to pay the price of using morally dubious means, or at least dangerous ones. As the sociologist concludes, the decisive means for politics is always violence. Again, to quote Weber, "He who seeks the salvation of soul, of his own and others, should not seek it along the avenue of politics, for the quite different tasks of politics can only be solved by violence. The genius or demon of politics lives in an inner tension with the God of Love, as well as with the Christian God as expressed by the Church."

What does the introduction of politics into religion do to the membership in the Church? Admittedly one cannot completely remove politics from a Church which is human. There will always be an attempt by some to influence leadership. What is the scurrilous deed in our day is the desire to manipulate teachings of what used to be called dogmas, for political purposes: power, gain, control over people.

What is being politicized are teachings: on the Eucharist, the obligations of community worship, the indissolubility of marriage, the primacy of the Pope. Christians are being pitted one against another about belief in these positions on the grounds of politics. Achievements of goals and ends, the setting up of classes, one against another, the whole ethnic/black confrontation have been brought into the Church as political issues, to make points against leadership, to win favor, to achieve positions for new leadership. It is not that these matters do not deserve consideration. Such problems must certainly come under the realm of justice and the social teaching of the Church. But it is the political area of these issues which is being stressed. With it has been the cessation of dialogue, the mounting clamor of shrill voices, the angry tone, the calling of names, and the increase of the lie at the expense of truth.

"Truthfulness," said Hannah Arendt, "has never been counted among the political virtues, and lies have always been regarded as justifiable tools in political dealings." She goes on: "The deliberate denial of factual truth—the ability to lie—and the capacity to change facts—the ability to act—are interconnected." It is the growth of violence, moral if not physical, and the lie that are sapping the strength both of the earthly city and Augustine's heavenly city—the People of God. We must valiantly resist and put another meaning to Christ's dictum: Give to Caesar (politics) what is political; but let us give to God what is God's —Christian faith, truth and love.

SOCIAL JUSTICE AND POLITICS

But in the post-Vatican II demands for social justice, a line between religion and ideology must be drawn. A smoldering wick which could lead to a powerful explosion in religion today lies hidden in the meaning of that phrase, "social justice." We are told that Fundamentalist churches are growing because of the discontent with the main Protestant bodies on that question. People are disillusioned with church leaders who have stressed social *causes* more than doctrinal elements. Such an accusation is made about the Church in the United States: that Church leaders and opinion-makers have gone too far in placing social projects high on priorities for action rather than the indoctrination and formation in faith of Christians. This is a thorny subject; one who tries to steer a middle course is condemned by the extreme sides. A middle course may be that the gospel makes strong demands for social justice; followers of Christ must in conscience work long and hard for a better kingdom here in a better world. But cannot it be argued that when specific programs are espoused, a move is made from pure gospel demand to ideology and politics. Then here Christians may freely disagree on the manner of action within a political context. We may become partisan; but our partisanship is not a matter of faith.

For example, Pat and Mike, both Catholics, believe and accept the Lord's injunction to care for and love the poor. They, in conscience, sincerely accept this obligation. Pat espouses the Democratic Party solution—e.g., he embraces Carter's welfare program. Mike, a Republican, believes that this program could contain more injustice than justice; he then works against that program, in favor of another. According to the gospel, which one is right? Here we move to the areas of an informed conscience. Father X may come and speak to Mike and point out that as a Catholic he is bound in conscience to work for the Democratic proposal. Father X may be exceeding his bounds, because he is espousing a program which is political, in which he believes as an individual. He is partisan. As a citizen, who is a Christian, that's okay. But as a priest he cannot order in faith. He may even be an expert in political science, in social activities, yet he cannot condemn Mike for a failure in Christianity. (The very same Catholic professionals who want freedom for individuals in questions of sexual morality, are the first to demand rigid acceptance of their own personal ideology and political program to achieve social justice.) The above Pat-Mike story may be challenged. Yet it seems to reflect Catholic teaching in morality.

Philosopher Michael Novak defends what he calls "democratic capitalism" in the July-August 1977 *Worldview*. Here, as a Catholic, he admits he may be taking an unpopular stand. Other Catholics, and especially some clerics and nuns (he mentions the Jesuit-staffed Center for Concern at Washington, D.C.), are pushing socialism as the only Christian way to achieve social justice, because to them it offers a truly humanistic view. Yet Novak asks some hard questions when he says, in the new socialist state they propose, who will be the planners? Who appoints them? What constituencies do they represent? Most of all, "what types of individuals will find fulfillment in such jobs?" He echoes what are the sentiments of some when he says: "That class of people most likely to be recruited as planners is not precisely the class to put most trust in."

On the other hand, Novak admits democratic capitalism has got problems. The American policy is not necessarily a good system. It is definitely not a Christian system. (Is there a Christian system of politics? No.) Our system may be inefficient, wasteful and ugly. But for Novak it is better than any known alternative. It is strange that the very people who have rejected Church authority line up for socialism, and demand that socialism exercise authority. Its task would be to plan and enforce their ideas; to restrict the ideas of others. One fact Novak holds as a basic tenet of democratic capitalism is this: the innate selfishness and corruptibility of every human being. He calls this "humanistic pessimism," and it is a saving doctrine. Everyone sometimes fails. Experience has taught us this. Once we knew this, we built in checks and balances into our system. We stress individual freedom and methods of trial and error. On the other hand, the doctrine of socialism makes two astounding assumptions, claims Novak, or acts of faith, if you will: 1) the individual can be liberated from the present institutions of society; 2) that liberated individual, no slave to self, will serve only the common good. People who have difficulty accepting scripture, in faith make these outrageous assumptions, forgetting that basic fact of human condition, original sin. Of which, alas, little is said. Novak cites Daniel Bell's greatest charge against democratic capitalism: it depends on the life of the spirit, which in practice it undercuts. Socialism in that sense, opposes religion, as a religion. Capitalism is no religion, no faith, but it needs the life of the spirit to counteract the materialism it pushes. This is our present dilemma. And here is where the professional teacher of religion is necessary. He is not to push, except as an opinion-maker, a citizen, a partisan, democratic capitalism or socialism. He cannot claim one or the other as the official Church teaching. A professional may do this privately and personally. But what he does best and should do is to bring back the things of the spirit, remind all of the need to be attuned to God's Word. These involve, necessarily and consistently, concern for the poor and the needy based on the gospel, the interior life and prayer as the wellsprings from which we draw our strength to do daily battle in the political arena. Here is where private enthusiasms or specific social programs as the only way to establish social justice may have undercut the very things we need to survive and to make God's kingdom come. What we must all do is to establish and keep alive our community of Faith, Hope and Charity.

But the social fabric, politics, these arise from our community concerns, our inter-relatedness. Even religion and the Church need that. But our anxiety is that we might be swallowed up, lost. Our tensions, then, in civic and religious society, arise from the conflict between the public person and the private.

COMMUNITY AND/VS. THE INDIVIDUAL

Years ago, when Svetlana Peters, Stalin's daughter who had married an American architect, left Taliesin West, a commune of "intellectuals" supervised by the wife of the late architect, Frank Lloyd Wright, she dramatized a conflict between "private" and "public." Svetlana's husband belonged to that commune, but she made an either/or demand on him, saying she would no longer live there because a flight from communal life (read: socialized life) was the reason she left Russia. Mrs. Peters said she wants to live her own private life.

The complexity of life creates tensions between the natural thrust of the human who must live in society, but wants to have some private moments.

This is nothing new. The demand to collectivize everything, to lump everything under one concept, is also part of man's nature. The medieval Arabian philosopher, Avicenna, proposed a doctrine of the "One Soul"—while bodies differ, human souls do not differ in essence or form. There is one world "Soul" for all. His contemporary, Averroes, went futher and spoke about the "agent Intelligence," which is one and the same for all mankind. From this came the conclusion: no man is immortal in himself, but somehow is caught up into the one immortality of the "agent Intellect." St. Thomas Aquinas reacted against both ideas, to insist on the individual's uniqueness and his individual immortality.

Presently in the Church there is an undercurrent of feeling expressed by some theologians that we must not press for personal immortality, or even for personal salvation. We are "saved" as one body. This cannot be explored yet because the concept depends on what they mean by these words, and meanings change from writer to writer.

The practical consequence of all this is the trend to the collectivization of spirituality, with a de-emphasis on private devotion and prayers, and of personal responsibility ("we are all guilty"). In this trend, we are not our own persons, but are caught up in the flow of the times.

Amitai Etzioni, a professor of sociology at Columbia University, spoke a few years ago at the Center for the Study of Democratic Institutions in California. One of our social currents, he saw, was the political-activist superculture where primacy is put on public life. All meaning is derived from public values. The danger, as he notes it, is that among other things, personal growth may be neglected. When questioned, Etzioni answered that he begins "with the individual having a nature of his own and a basic set of needs which no society can tamper with." When he was challenged by the late John Cogley, who was arguing for the primacy of social values, and who claimed that Etzioni was making society a metaphysical identity distinct from its members, the sociologist reiterated his fear of any society "which imposes its goal on its members." Better first to discover what goals individuals want.

This, it seems, may have been and continues to be the chief problem of these decades: a basic struggle in which either individuals will be completely lost in society, or the individual rights shall triumph over those needs which men can only fulfill when they work together in society.

One does grow weary of public preachers and teachers who insist that individuals must conform to some pre-determined brand of spirituality, the current "in" brand of prayer or liturgical life—or, in short, of those who impose their goals on the members of the Church. What may be lacking today is the means for individuals within the Church to express what each truly wants. That this is no easy matter is admitted. The idea that there is some kind of a super group which knows what is good for all the members, must be avoided—whether it be bishops, theologians, social activists, liturgists, columnists or whatever. It was that kind of mentality which has succeeded, to some extent, in driving out the rosary, medals, statues, etc., some of which certain individuals needed as part of their religious expression. Equally to be avoided is the attempt to establish personal likes and dislikes as a common denominator by which all public and devotional acts within the Church are to be judged.

You see the paradox and the problem? Either we risk the danger of losing individuals in the collective mass, or we will not be able to create a community of belief because of the victory of individual preferences over what we can and must do together. It's complicated, yet this may be the battle of the eighties.

Still the question has not been clearly delineated. Why? The word "institution" is now pejorative and is always contrasted with the "individual," as if they were contradictory.

INDIVIDUAL VS. INSTITUTION

A few years ago *Time* magazine reported a rebirth of interest in the medieval period. Courses on this era are being offered in colleges and universities, and eager students sign up to learn about medieval history, art, philosophy, culture. At Western Michigan University the annual medieval seminar exceeds past attendance. Benedictine and Cistercian scholars conduct courses there. Many museums display the perennial beauty of painting, artifacts, sculpture of the period. Sold-out concerts feature medieval "consorts" with programs specializing in music of the Middle Ages. Medieval study is IN. (Except with some Catholic scholars, who are probably into Marxism.)

The question is, why? Is this a flight from the sterile, mass-produced, anti-life plastic culture of our day? Is it a search, by return to values of what were days of "faith," even if that "faith" were overlaid with too much credulity? Thoughts particularly addressed to this question, but which provide insight are expressed by that unusual author, William Irwin Thompson. In a chapter, "The Individual as Institution" (contained in a book, *Passages about Earth: An Exploration of the New Planetary Cultures*), Professor Thompson, philosopher, anthropologist, student of literature and history, and founder of a new educational and religious center, the Lindisfarne Association, spoke of a return to the "medieval image" as a return to the values of order, or as he said, going "from secular disintegration to sacral re-integration."

Thompson's basic concern is the conflict between individual and institution. He cites Paolo Soleri, artist and architect, who is trying in the western United States to create a new style of living: anti-urban, a mixture of architecture and "arcology," which rejects our sprawling extended megalopolis for a new city life that is intense, simplified, central, with "living room." For all men cannot live in the desert or wilderness; the city must be the humanizing influence. In the city Soleri finds the written word, music, art, and relationships between men. The city makes "community," but the city also makes "institution," and the problem arises in the tension between "community" and "institution." Not our technological city; a new kind of city.

Today the Catholic Church calls for "community," "the people of God," as a collective. This is accepted, even praised. But when the Church as institution tries to give guidelines in faith as to who constitutes community, it is denounced for behaving as institution.

William Irwin Thompson, once a Catholic, proclaims that the modern problem is that of power. He sees the Church as beginning with the use of power to help men prepare for eternity; but that use ended up as authoritarian. Such authority-power was good in the medieval period. It is not so good now.

The author quotes an interesting distinction made by Soleri who said, "I have no *power* over my students. They are free to come and go. I have only *authority*. If they come to me because of my authority, and they do not respect that authority, they have no reason for coming to work with me. Authority has the power of conviction. Authoritarianism has the power of coercion." Authority convinces; authoritarianism coerces.

The greater paradox involves the individual versus and within institution. The Middle Ages brought about the emergence of the masses, the "people," the "folk." In this process, the "individual" emerged seeking to be free from the aristocracy, from the tribe, from communal religious restrictions. Now we are at the end of that process in our modern world. It would appear we are dashing towards collectivization, uniformity, the non-distinctive modern man.

Thompson believes Teilhard de Chardin regarded this process as good. He quotes the Jesuit:

"Although our individualistic instincts may rebel against this drive toward the collective, they do so in vain and wrongly." Why vain? No worldly power can help us escape from the power of the world. And wrongly, this impulse really moving us to super-organization makes us more personalized and human.

Does it? We are in McLuhan's "world as a tribal village." And we want to hearken back to individual worth, individual value, individual dignity. The proponents of consumer participation, present mind-expanding gurus, and all those others who want the individual to rediscover himself are objecting to such a corporate concept of humanity. It is evidenced by the disaffection of the young with technology, with the political process, with conglomerates, all failing to accommodate to the needs of the individual. We are in a quasi-religious movement, a new secular monasticism, a "quietism" ("personal" religion), and Eastern mysticism, a turning in on oneself, brought about by rejection of corporate humanity.

What this could mean for the Church has been revealed already in the disaffection with those portions of the new liturgy as communal, collective. Some people seek out smaller, more relating groups, not so much an elitism as a search for personal relationships and individual meanings. When this fails, as it must do, then the disenchantment may lead to a removal of self from the "community of believers," to a "personal religion," the "God within me."

We in the Church have not made up our mind. We stress the corporate, the "pilgrim Church," but we seek individual leaders for personal needs, personal rewards. For the Church, this may mean that Church leaders must seek to reestablish "authority." They must demonstrate knowledge and qualifications that will lead people to come willingly and to eschew power as power.

Our modern view is to "collectivize" everything—even our dislikes, our failures. We want to bind or be bound together—we who do not want to fit into a "mass," to proclaim our individual worth and self.

Who will help us? Those leaders who remind us that Christ said each of us, not all of us, is more precious than the sparrow, the field lilies. There are not too many who tell us that today. Be like the "Church," they say, but until I am myself, I cannot ever be like the Church. We want rather to be as the Father is, holy.

One of the most unexplained of modern phenomena—mobility—may have hastened the process of distintegration of old forms and styles for newer ones. Somebody might (possibly has) do a research paper on mobility and its influence on the Church—its institutions, its personnel, its programs.

MOBILITY

Question: Is it merely advancing age or does it seem each year that winter comes upon us more threatening than before? The feeling may be due to the proliferation of TV and weather forecasters who scare us on Sundays about the terrible blasts of weather which may or may not happen the following Friday. Some of the uneasiness may come from new techniques adopted by weather bureaus which issue "travelers' warnings" (who isn't a traveler these days?). The fact may derive from the growing number of cars and the aggravation caused by chemicals which melt highway snow but mess up cars, vision, and people.

For the sake of discussion, is the villain of such winter weariness mobility? Never has any society in the world at any point in history as ours, felt it so necessary almost each and every day to be somewhere else within ever shorter periods of time. Big business now lives on trips by scores of uniformly dressed young and middle-aged men, flocking to the airports early in the morning to scatter hither and yon on the great winged birds to conclude business deals, but who want to be back in their homes later that evening. Other professions thus challenged, respond by meetings at those new abominations, plasticized high-rise motels situated close to the airport, to which people flock by plane from all parts of the country. There they drink impossible coffee, smoke innumerable cigarettes, consider weighty problems, and digest routine food which adds to the weightiness by all that sitting around. Almost every day someone has to go to Washington, Chicago, Houston, New York, Louisville, Los Angeles, to meet with other people who really don't want to be there. All must listen to "show and tell," packaged programs, come up with instant solutions and super-efficient courses of action. But this must be done within two hours, so that the long, wearying journey back can begin—if the plane is on time and not snowbound.

The restlessness of our day contributes much to our need for mobility. No one wants to stay home anymore. Father Manton's classical definition of home as "the place you go to when all the other places are closed" has been verified. Evenings bring high school basketball games, cheer leader meetings, CCD classes, and various other gatherings to and from which children and adults must be transported. Cultural events come trooping one after another—balls and bazaars, symphonies and ballets, rock concerts, and excursions into nostalgia, expensively priced, of course, as are so many other divertissements to wean us away from home and hearth.

Who wants to stay home anymore of an evening? Who wants to curl up with a good book, when without any exercise of endeavor one can see shadowy characters on movie screens? Yes, you can stay home, but quickly become bored with the same but later shown characters on TV screens. If there is no special children's TV room, these young demand to watch programs with much noise, shouting and shooting. The only alternative to TV is to turn it off, to begin talking to one another. Who is prepared to do that in an age when we have lost the art of conversation, when "argument" no longer means civilized debate but a succession of cliches, or assaults on personal integrity? Who wants to stay home when there are so many interesting reasons to get out of it?

So, mobility. We are a people on the move. We grab our meals, gulp them. We thrive on franchised foods, instant meals, a process of ingestion that will not keep us in one place longer than necessary. To move, one needs roads and good weather. Consequently winter now has become neither our old-time friend, bearer of white snow which reminds us of the old days on the farm (that we never had, but long for), nor an enemy that threatens to engulf us with high snow banks and isolate us so that we can be cut off from it all. Winter, mostly in cities and nearby, then becomes a nasty, dirty, messy inconvenience, adding still more hassles to our already hassled life, and anxieties to our over-anxious selves. There are snow tires, windshield scrapers, getting the car washed more often, keeping up to date on the weather reports, having a supply of rags to clean the windshield, hoping as we begin that the road ahead has neither ice nor glaze, watching out for the guy ahead to see if he makes the hill, and generally making our need to be mobile an unpleasant experience.

Yet, fall and winter become the busy times for churches. Council meetings, CCD, Adult Discussion, "Enrichment" Programs, Study Clubs, Drives, Seminars, Conventions—all places to get to. So mobility involves church business.

The solution? Who knows? Perhaps the place to begin is to say no to meetings, to discourage unnecessary trips, to find reasons to stay home with the family instead of to flee from it, to curtail our excursions outside.

Possibly husbands and wives can start experiments in talking to each other, discovering mutual interests, returning to the lost art of reading, and even to that Victorian joy of reading aloud to one's children or to one another.

Perhaps as in so many other things, the home is at the heart of the solution. Isn't it ironic that the best-selling homes today are "mobile" homes? They match the mood of a people who unwillingly are forced indoors for the night, and can hardly wait to start out again.

As a consequence we have the energy crisis development. All the previous is exacerbated. We dare not be kept in any one place. That would literally be deadly. Little wonder then that the urge comes on us every so often to disappear, to get out of sight, to get lost, to go "incognito."

INCOGNITO

Father Frederic Debuyst, of St. Andrew's Abbey in Belgium, editor of the quarterly *Art d'Eglise,* once wrote "A Eulogy of the Incognito." This Benedictine's specialty seems to be to look at the ordinary in an extraordinary manner, as a result of which it appears in a new, fresh and different light.

Incognito: there's a word we've used so often

without really looking at it. It comes from a Latin word meaning "unknown." Usually it is applied to mean "hiding one's identity." For Dom Frederic it is a manner of being which hides great inner richness behind a modest exterior, which, he thinks, is true for buildings as well as persons. That's not all: to plumb that inner richness, to search out the inner "effulgence" is what makes a man or object cease being "incognito" and by which it reveals its real self.

Father Debuyst relates this concept to two other themes he has dwelt upon before: celebration, the intimacy of a true feast, and the walk, the journey, the trip which is within, as well as without. At once the priest thinks of Christ on the road to Emmaus (three men on a trip, men who in the journey find their inner selves—"Did not our hearts burn as we talked with Him?") with the aid of the unknown companion (Christ traveling incognito), and especially in the feast, the breaking of the bread. Christ's face, unrecognized by them, became familiar, as what is within was revealed by day's end. So too with us, concludes the monk. Before we can affirm what we are by our face, we must make our own private journey from within to outside, until we learn to recognize ourselves, and then allow the world to see us as we truly are.

To do this is much against the spirit of the times. We are snatched up in the culture of the spectacle, of the show, of the instant outward impact, in conclusions to be drawn from quick, fast, simultaneous perception (the TV syndrome). Note the growth of the kind of theater which demands audience participation: the audience, and individuals in it, become the show. Individuals are lost in the collective; units are smothered up in the totality. No one is content anymore to let things be revealed gradually. There is no time, all must be shown at once, in the 30-second or one-minute commercial, the half-hour show, the one-night stand. Above all, allow no man time to learn about himself. Use lights, sound, color, drugs—anything to reveal the inner abysses instantaneously. Or if you are afraid that inside you there is only a void, the vacuum within, then falsify, project another image, not the self you are, but a self you think the world wants to see. Hence the schizoid, the disjunctive living of our day.

What is needed so much is time to withdraw, to discover the "incognito," to search out the hidden being. We must, in the words of Peguy, limit ourselves to giving "just enough of presence, and just enough of absence." Husbands and wives, lovers, families must separate once in a while to discover the self.

Scripture seems to bless the incognito. "When you give, let your alms be in secret, so that the Father, Who sees in secret, will reward." Prayer must also be at times incognito. "When you pray, go into your room, and shut the door and pray to your Father Who is in secret." So many times Jesus demands sincerity of heart, the "inner" regard, directed to God and self, and not to the judgments of men. To put it philosophically, we must discover our "being," which is hidden (even to ourselves) behind the "appearing."

This reveals the sudden (but always ready) need of human beings today for the "private place," the place for withdrawal, the place for meditation (natural or religious). It may be the den, where a man may be himself, the kitchen nook, and the morning cup of coffee where the housewife can find and draw upon her inner resources; the "place apart" where the world stands outside, while the self discovers who and what it is. It can be a quiet corner, a small space in the public library, a toolshed, a hobby room, the basement room where the world shrinks down to that space in which a human being can discover himself. It can be the field, the valley, the mountain, the seashore, the oceans, where nature is always "incognito," waiting to be discovered in its hidden and changing moods.

It used to be the parish church—the "visit." It used to be the possibility to slip away for a few moments for a talk before the Eucharist (what better incognito, where both Master and servant are hidden, and the inner-ness of both must reach out to new discovery). But that seems to be lost and must be rediscovered again.

We have put so much store on the communitarian aspect of the liturgy. We have come to think that this, and only this, is the official, valid prayer of men. We forget that all liturgy began in a quiet corner of Gethsemane, in the small "upper room."

Incognito is summarized in a quote from Louis Lavelle, "Wisdom is the ability to keep constant the facility of remaining close to the most secret center of one's soul from which joy is always ready to spring up." There is joy in discovering self, rediscovering ever anew. Take some time off, today. Go out in search of yourself. Look for the incognito which you must discover, if you are going to be true to your possibilities, to your being.

But we look for more in our "incognito" search. We really want space, personal space, growing space.

SPACE

John Hersey's *My Petition for More Space* was a fantasy projected into a not-too-distant future time when there is no more space in the world. His short novel considered what could happen when people in a large American city begin destroying others in a demand for more space. By design a horror tale, it was also a plea for population control, a scare story to promulgate what Hersey sees as the indiscriminate begetting of the human species. It never took off in the book world.

Against this background there are the thoughts of Donald Nicholl (London *Tablet,* 1/11/75) recalling Kabbalistic teaching (the Kabbala is a book of Jewish mysticism of the late medieval and early renaissance period). According to the Kabbala, God created all things in a special fashion. He withdrew into Himself (the Hebrew word is "tsimtsum"—that is, withdrawing), and by such withdrawal, God made space for other things, the rest of the world, creation, including us. By "tsim-tsum" God gave to men life, space and time.

Although we are in the "space age," ironically space is becoming a premium. Humans crowd into development projects, they stand in line at super-markets, department stores, and gasoline stations on weekends. The problem is less serious in rural America than it might be, for example, in metro-politan areas. Or less serious in America than in tight little islands like England, where in urban centers such as London, people literally have no space in which to breathe.

Yet Nicholl points out that we are being pushed in another way for space. From the moment we get up, many people are clamoring in different ways for our space. They want to fill our space with their thoughts and ideas. They seek to preempt our minds, to put themselves (their opinions and views) into it. Case in point: the average American hears the same set of news, supposedly "factual," 8, 10, 15 times a day. These "news" reports originate from the same sources, the accredited news wires or central news systems. News reporters read these on radio and TV as if they were just new, even though they may have been read (and heard) many times that day. By the end of the day, our mind-space has been swallowed up by other's "facts." We know more than we need or care to know. But by then, little or no space has been left for us.

Against space-gobblers, consider those who seek to give us space. These are the artists, those who have created musical masterpieces, works of literature, poetry, great art, and all those spaces in which we can find our own selves each day, or any day we want, throughout our lives. Blessed be such space-makers. Instead of making our space theirs, they allow us to rediscover our personal space in their creations. In a sense, they are doing what God did—by "tsimtsum," they are making space for us by withdrawing (pulling away from their works), giving them to us, so that we can have room to be.

It is probable there are more who want to rob our space than there are space-makers today. This could even be true in the Church. The landscape of religion is cluttered with people who do not wish to give us information to make our own decisions, as much as to propagandize, to make us their satellites, to sell their point of view. By devices of propaganda, it is their intention to make of us mere puppets, empty echoes of themselves. In a sense, they want to stuff us into them, swallow up our space, and not allow us to be different from them. But this is not religion. It is scarcely God-like (or of God), Who by His withdrawing has let us be our own individual selves. Instead of "tsimtsum," such propagandists are doing just the opposite. They seek to expand their space, and allow no room for others to have space.

It's odd how the myths about people occupying our space (our individuality) have become perpetuated in monster movies and stories. There is the "zombie" who is not himself, but somebody else's slave. There is the monster created by new

Doctor Frankensteins who seek to assert in others their own individualities. There are myths of werewolves and vampires whose bite transforms others, and who take over another's personality. We are fascinated with these stories because they express a fear deeply hidden within ourselves. We want to be; we want to be individuals; we are afraid of people moving into our bodies and minds.

It is precisely this concept that needs to be expounded. If we allow more space for others, we allow more space for ourselves. This is the dilemma of our day. We need to reject the temptation to occupy the space of others. We need to discover our own space. That may be task enough. Let us make times and places, by withdrawing into our own spheres of control, for others to be.

Finally, as Nicholl says, we need prayer. Prayer is nothing else but withdrawing into self, as God did, and allowing room for God to be, about us and within us. Perhaps we ought to recite a new prayer: Blessed are the space-makers, for they shall find themselves. In so doing, may they find the God Who gave them the space to be.

ANTICIPATION

But in our mobility, lack of space, the hustle and hassle, many things have been destroyed. Consider "anticipation," that very human and once wonderful experience. Anticipation, we were told, carried as much joy and happiness as did the fulfillment of what was anticipated. In fact, some said anticipation was better than fulfillment. It flavored the on-coming moment with the promise of gratification, with the enjoyable fantasies of looked-forward-to hopes.

Anticipation was particularly a great part of the childhood experience. The anticipation of holi-days, and their special joys; the looking forward with joy to the end of school and the vacation period; the waiting out of days to the school picnic; graduation; birthdays; the senior prom—all these were moments to be savored in the expectancy as much as the completion.

But anticipation was also a happiness of adult-hood. There were the Sunday dinners, once such a part of American culture; the family feasts; the an-nual vacation; the stages of the ritual passage of children to adulthood, long pants, first nylons, first job, first paycheck, first child.

Religious rituals spoke of anticipation as a blessed gift from God. It was a way the Creator had allowed us to enjoy even more the happiness of certain moments and events in the pilgrimage through life from birth to death, and on to the Eter-nal City (Heaven, not Rome).

Is it wrong to say that anticipation has become a fearsome monster? Consider merely any ap-proaching holiday. How many adults live each day not in joy of anticipation, but in the fear and hatred of holidays? Each day advertisers stress what must yet be done in the days before Christ-mas (Mother's Day, Valentine's Day, etc.). Excori-ated by the reminder that precious time is running out, people get guilt feelings because they have not acted earlier and so will find only picked-over merchandise, things no longer available. The implications all around are that you are a poor parent, a bad housewife, a deficient breadwinner if a thousand and one things are not done by you to make each holiday super-special for all in the family. So each day of almost any season is fraught with horror as the time runs out, like some judgment waiting for us: will the days come to find us wanting?

Anticipation has become the prerogative of the press, aggravated by the need of magazines and newspapers to grind out stories. Stories begin to appear in early September about Christmas planning, and from that moment on, the aggravating season is on until the Christmas holiday goes (the day after).

The changed face of anticipation is not only the case in the holidays. Parents are now getting used to the fact that if they want their children to go to college, they must plan ahead. Such planning means that Junior must get good marks in the 5th and 6th grades of elementary school. For parents as well as for Junior, anticipation of that happy day of college entrance becomes rather a cloud hanging over the head. Will he make it? In which college will he be accepted? Will we have the money? Start saving now in our college-investment plan, say the banks. And what should be a normal human experience becomes a slow exercise in torture.

The summer vacation must be planned in January. First Dad has to cut out his time slot for vacation according to the company schedule. Next, if there's any kind of a trip, reservations must be made "well in advance," and thus begins another round of anxieties of anticipation.

When you go journeying for holidays, you must begin a day or two in advance "in order to escape the rush." Make motel reservations well in advance. Do this, do that. Who needs it?

It happens all around in many ways. Whether it is the increase of the tempo of our times, or the terrible stress on "planning ahead," it adds up to little or no joy. Thus what should have been happier moments in life become so filled with such unhappiness from the mounting annoyances, that when the moment of fulfillment arrives, all one can say is, "Thank God it's over." Only to be followed by, "But we had better begin planning now for next year."

Perhaps we ought to get back to another Christian maxim of living each day at a time. You know, "sufficient to the day . . . ." Or so at least we think on the "bad days." Are there any other? But how can I accept somebody ordering me to "have a good day," when I know, I just know, I'm going to have a bad day?

BAD DAYS

Newspapers occasionally trot out a feature story of "Biorhythm," a pseudo-scientific theory which holds that each person, according to his physical structure, has his own fluctuating periods of high activity and negative activity. The idea is that the individual, keeping accurate daily records of physical activities, will soon discover that there are periods within a month when he is at the height of creativity, and other times when his creativity is at its lowest ebb. These productive periods, according to "biorhythm," have something to do with metabolism, circulation, sleep and so on.

The theory catches hold of a truth; many of us recognize there may be something to it. We know from personal experience that on certain days everything goes right. We get lots done; we make the right decisions; we sparkle; move efficiently; and achieve greatly. But then there are those other times: the days "we should have stayed in bed." Nothing goes right. Is it a matter of blood pressure, metabolism, physical "rightness?" Or is it something more? Are the "days" themselves troublesome: Fridays, the 13th of a month, Mondays?

In the medieval period, long before "biorhythm," that was the explanation. There were some days that of themselves were unlucky. It was held there were two days each month when no business should be transacted. No one should drink on those days, travel, or "be bled" by doctors. They were called "Egyptian days" ("dies aegyptiaci"), probably because such unlucky days were first calculated by Egyptian astrologers. Others saw the name from the scripture text of the plagues called down on Pharaoh and the Egyptians by Moses, "when there was a thick darkness in all the land of Egypt for three days."

Egyptian astrologers had the reputation of knowing their business. They did draw up a list of lucky days and bad days "on which there was a struggle in the world between good and evil."

But the name for these days was the best: they were called "dismal." The word is French, "dis mal," from the Latin "dies mali," evil or unlucky days. In England, to say "in the dismal" was to mean "at an unlucky time," "in evil days." In time, the original meaning was forgotten. "Dismal" became an adjective and people spoke of "dismal days," which was really saying twice: "in evil days days."

Churchmen in the 16th century saw all this about "bad days" as superstition and an affront to God. Did not God make all days good? Why were some days prejudged to be bad? "Dismal," in time, grew weaker and weaker, moving from "disaster" and "sinister," to merely "dreary" and "cheerless."

Now, as "biorhythm" seeks to tell us, it is not in the fault of the day, or our stars, but it lies in our physical well-being. Not everybody has the same "bad days." You may be up, while I am down, and vice-versa. Learn your "biorhythm" and you can use this knowledge to good effect. But we still don't trust Fridays, or Mondays, or "the 13th day." Other religious-minded people will consult the different astrology and Zodiac tables in the daily papers and magazines, and act accordingly.

("Don't make a decision from the 14th to the 21st of this month.") But possibly from our common dim past, whenever we break a glass, spill the coffee, slam a door on our fingers, we just say, "I guess this isn't my lucky day."

Alas, it seems sometimes there are just too many of those days around. Or so one would guess if one listened to a rather peculiar tone of our days.

CARPING

This strange tone or spirit seems rampant. The word "carping" suits it, or "nitpicking." We all know the adage, "You can't please everybody." In current opinion anybody can do the other fellow's job better. It is also a fact that everybody knows where his neighbor, superior, friend did wrong. No one ever says what the other person may have done right. "Carping" comes from the Scandinavian "carpen," to wrangle. There does seem to be much unnecessary wrangling.

These thoughts were prompted by the well-deserved exasperation of a priest who believed that some persons (his parishioners? his peers? brother priests?) expressed a carping attitude about a program instituted by the priest. They said more should be done. Yet by his planning and diligence, great good had already been achieved. The priest-friend sighed, for instance, and said, "Probably when the Lord Jesus multiplied the loaves and fishes, although the Gospel does not mention this, there were possibly some disciples who said to a few of the by-standers, but not to the Lord, 'That's fine, feeding all those people. But did you notice he didn't tell us what he was going to do with those twelve baskets of fragments left over? He will no doubt keep them for some of his special friends. I would bet he'd give them to Lazarus and Mary and Martha. They don't need it. I know a couple of poor families who could certainly use those leftovers more than that family.' "

Maybe the priest was right. It could be that the gospels do not tell us the full story. Some gospel incidents come to mind and in that vein, the follow-up may not have been reported by the evangelists.

Was there a critic in the wings at the time of the Magi who said: "The gold we can use. But what can anybody do with frankincense and myrrh? There's just no market for that. Why didn't they make their gifts all gold and be done with it? I suspect they have some stock in the Star of Jerusalem Incense and Myrrh Company."

When Jesus was discovered teaching in the temple at the age of 12, did the religious law experts, aides to those doctors of the law with whom Jesus had exchanged dialogue, say: "Did you notice how that young fellow didn't stick by the book we put out? Did you notice how he kept wanting to put his own opinions in, instead of listening to us? We went off to the Jerusalem University and got our degrees in religious teaching of the Torah. What has he done? A smart young fellow like that could upset our whole program with the young. Maybe we ought to talk to his parents and tell them he can't come back until he changes his attitude toward us."

Did Peter's mother-in-law, who was cured of fever by Jesus, say after the Lord was out of hearing, "It's all very well, yes he cured me, he had to. He knows somebody has to take care of this house and my daughter while my son-in-law, that Peter, is traipsing all over the country instead of fishing for a living as he should. Jesus can go roaming, he has no wife and family to look after. The thing this Rabbi should have done was tell Peter to stay at home with his family."

When Jesus walked on the water and Peter tried but began to sink, was there someone in the boat who said: "See, he wants to keep that secret to himself. He's afraid if we learn the trick he'll have lost the advantage of leadership. If we knew how to do that, just think, we could open a school and make some money, which of course we would give to him but only after we took out our teachers' salaries. the cost of the boats and the clothes that will probably be ruined in the training period."

When the Lord cured the daughter of the Syro-Phoenician woman, was there a woman in the crowd who said: "Well, yes, he cured the girl but did he have to insult that woman? You heard what he said. He practically called her a dog. He said something about it not being lawful to give bread which belongs to the children of Israel to foreigners, and something about the crumbs. No, I tell you he didn't have to treat her that roughly—that was a typical male trick."

How about the man by the Bath of Bethsaida, did he tell someone after he was cured: "Well, that's fine but I have been sitting around by this pool for 12 years. Why did it take this Jesus so long to get here? Just think of the good things I have missed and the fun I could have had in those 12 years."

Did the owner of the house, through whose roof the friends of the paralytic lowered him to be cured by Christ, end up the whole incident by saying: "Okay, now who's going to pay for the roof?"

Maybe the gospels are idealized versions of what men can be. Probably some souls even then were carping about the Lord. Still, you would hope that somebody, just somebody, today appreciated what God accomplished through His people, weak and sinful as they are. Maybe not all of the good has been done yet, not all the poverty wiped away, not all greed, jealousy and envy removed from the hearts of men. Some people try in small steps, but they try. Because they are creatures they can't make it a perfect work, nor accomplish it all. Yet shouldn't we be happy, even despite our imperfections, that God still allows and helps us to do some good? And stop the carping?

Or is it, as some believe, our sour spirit arises from another source: we had our expectations raised much too high and suddenly found it wasn't going to happen that way. But we were going to beat all that poverty and racism and enslavement of people, weren't we? We could do it. We could win. But we didn't. It's all still out there.

NORBERT GAUGHAN

LOSERS

So President Ford was right one way in his anti-inflation speech. He chose the magic American word "WIN" as his catchphrase. We love that word. America loves winners and hates losers. The pro football season gives us winners. Collegians try football not only for alma mater, for if they win, there is a lifetime career in a multi-million dollar business. They can then make fortunes, not for personal worth or value, but only as "winners" to be exploited in TV, radio, the press, to push "winning" products.

But is winning so great? This need to win may be at the base of all our troubles. We believe America is a winning country—i.e., a country of winners. The Vietnamese war was not won by us (nor, they tell us, did we lose it). We just "pulled out." We can't allow ourselves to lose to inflation; WIN we must!

Our children from early age are taught the necessity to win—that is, to get ahead. Ahead of whom? Ahead of others. Ahead of our class, ahead of our peers, ahead of the other kids and other adults in the block. If you get ahead, you're a winner.

There is only one alternative in our American lexicon to winning, that is, to lose. No in-betweens are allowed. If you're not a winner, you are a loser. But that's just not true. Why? Because we do not choose at what to win; it is set by our culture, by our mores, by our national mood. Some things are not worth winning in America's values, so don't mention them. To win at being the kindest, most gentle person is not noteworthy. To win at being a good man, a kind husband, a loving father, well, that is expected. No allowances are made for a woman to be the best kind of person she can be. She must excel in secretaryship, politics, causes, beauty, competitons, or Women's Lib.

We need a new patron saint for America, or at least a secondary patron. Why not promote national devotion to St. Joseph the Just? Now you may ask, who is St. Joseph the Just? No, it is not the popular St. Joseph, the foster father of Christ. St. Joseph the Just is better known as Joseph Barsabbas, son of Sabbas. We know very little about him. Butler's *Lives of the Saints* gives him a short paragraph. There are no extended records of his martyrdom, no trace of missionary activity on his part. He does exemplify precisely the reason we should honor him. For Joseph the Just was a loser.

Who is he? He is mentioned in the Acts of the Apostles (Acts I, 23), where he is given the name "Justus." He was placed in a competition for the office of "apostle," opened by the self-inflicted death of Judas Iscariot. Joseph Justus was probably one of the 72 disciples associated with the Lord (Acts I, 21). Joseph's rival was Matthias. The election was decided not on merit (both Joseph and Matthias must have been equally worthy to be so considered), but by the Holy Spirit. They drew lots. We do not know what kinds of lots. Was it broom straws, the short one losing, the long one winning?

Whatever, we do not know. But by divine election Matthias was declared a winner. Joseph the Just became a loser. Or was he? Matthias "took rank with the 11 Apostles," Joseph went on to be forgotten. Yet, who was the true winner? Was Matthias the best man for the role of apostle? Or was Joseph the lesser man for the job? We do not know; scripture adds little. Joseph did go on to be a winner in the one thing he should have been a winner and that is, in being what God wanted him, Joseph, to be, and that was not an apostle, but a Christian.

It is sad that others determine for us at what we shall win or lose. In the Church, misguided people congratulate a bishop and say, "I hope you go on to become a cardinal, or an archbishop, or a pope." (If he doesn't, he's a loser.) Some think the greatest compliment they can pay a priest is to say, "Well, I hope you're a bishop." They may be, on the basis of the Peter Principle, dooming him. All these are externals, for what the individual priest must be is the best he can at being a priest according to his talents and his limitations. If he does that, he has won, not in the worldly sense, but in the truer sense. So too with any Christian, any task.

Back in the 30s we had a Church of winners. We count Cardinal Newman, G. K. Chesterton, Ronald Knox in England, all winners. (Knox never made bishop.) We had Fulton Sheen, who was making "winning" converts everywhere, such as Clare Boothe Luce and Henry Ford. Now we are a Church of "losers," it is claimed. People of good mind and some sensibilities have elected to leave the Church for diverse reasons. They ("good minds," we are told, i.e., winners) say, "I want to get out," and thereby declare that the Catholic Church is a losing proposition. We have had losses not only of numbers and "good minds" in people of promise and ability, but of some who could have helped in the mission of the Church. The Church appears to be a church of losers. In America it has lost some Supreme Court decisions. Catholics have wasted away the respect and admiration (if we ever had it) of some TV people and important publishers. Scarcely a week goes by but someone gleefully reports that some important personage ("a winner") has left the Church.

Such talk is nonsense. The spirit to win is indeed keen. But winning is not all that important, at least not in those races which are declared important by the princes and powers of this world. Our Lord Jesus declared winnning as "saving your soul." He said that we might have to face up to the fact that this kind of winning comes only after defeat, after the princes and powers of this world have declared that we are non-essential, non-important, non-winners.

Could some enterprising priest prepare for us a litany (another loser, litanies) in honor of St. Joseph the Just, St. Joseph the Loser? Might we have a novena (another losing proposition these instantaneous days) in honor of St. Joseph the Just? Could we have inspiring sermons on the proposition that the American ideal of winning is all wrong, based as it is on false assumptions, on the values and judgments of this world? Could we all begin to be satisfied to be losers in this world, in order to win peace of soul, clear consciences, and integrity? That may mean no compromise here, in order to achieve happiness hereafter.

ST. JOCK

Nowhere is that desire of ours to win more apparent than in our "cult of St. Jock." This especially reveals how permissive have become our language habits. Words once restricted to smoking rooms or in the "for men only" category are now used by all, with no restrictions save good taste. (But since that phrase "good taste" is synonymous to many with mere Victorian manners, that means there are no restrictions at all.)

Consider the word "jock." In 17th century English it was used as a euphemism for the private parts of the human body, male or female. At the beginning of a later, athletic-minded century (our own), it was used as an adjective to describe a piece of athletic equipment used by men in more strenuous sports.

Now "jock" has come to full term as a noun. "Jocks" are athletes, professional more or less, who play at sports for a living, as a major preoccupation, or with great emphasis on that kind of endeavor. "Jock" is used in book titles, in descriptive commentary, in conversations of every kind. Little wonder, since it describes our phenomenon: the adulation, even worship, given to athletic prowess. It was ever thus; masters of brawn and proficiency in muscular contests have always been respected throughout history. But it has been our contribution to introduce a new element: the deliberate exaltation of this aspect of human activity of promoters seeking to derive from it large quantities of money. Rightfully such entrepreneurs have gauged the public temper. We are definitely in a "bread or circuses" mood; we need diversion from the daily round of bad news and crises that inundate our lives. We need entertainment; but plays, movies, concerts are not accepted by all. In fact, by some they are considered "sissified" forms of recreation. What men need, the belief goes, is mainly entertainment. Hence, sports, sports, sports.

The word "worship" is not employed lightly. We are truly worshipping at the shrine of St. Jock. In an age of the decline of Catholic magazines, and the falling off of the secular press, it is interesting to note, as reported by Publishers Information Bureau, the remarkable growth of "jock" magazines, such as *Golf Digest, Ski, Field and Stream, Sports Illustrated.* This is due not merely to a matter of leisure interest. These magazines provide a new kind of spiritual writing. They detail stories and anecdotes, much like the lives of the saints of old, about the new heroes worshipped by the multitude.

In fact, the cultic worship theme is not too far out. St. Jock has his temples. Notice the ever-larger, ever-newer stadia being built across the

land to accommodate the throngs of eager wor-
shippers. The center of each stadium no longer
relies on nature's coverings; it is lovingly carpeted
with turf of new plastic materials that will be
proper to the sacred rites performed thereon. The
stadia are well lit. St. Jock's cult is best followed in
rituals that wait upon the nighttime. The acolytes
and ministers vary: from the promoters who initi-
ate the rites, through the referees and attendants
who see that the sacred ritual is properly carried
out according to the rubrics, down to the lowliest
menial who hawks peanuts and programs so that
the faithful may be properly fed and instructed.

There are even vestments. One "Today" show
carried a segment describing the changes in baseball clothes through the decades to today's flashy,
streamlined, form-fitting styles. A religion is no
good without its prophets. St. Jock has his: the
varied but many sports announcers, newspaper
writers, journalists and hangers-on who seek to
whip up interest in support of the local rites in the
great St. Jock. The cult has its helps to devotion:
liniments which become its holy water; various accessories, belts, bandages, and cleats to help the
hero achieve the heights of sanctity demanded by
the populace. It also has its heretics: those who
depart disillusioned and write books in the manner
of Jim Bouton, showing how the heroes of St. Jock
have clay feet. It has sinners: homosexual athletes,
dope-takers, etc. There is a liturgical year also. St.
Jock of the Baseball Diamond reigns from Febru-
ary to October; St. Jock of the Gridiron holds sway

from August to January; St. Jock of the Basketball Court presides from October to April. Hockey—practically all year around. Holydays are observed in January (New Year's Day and the second Sunday of January are high holydays), July and October.

There are some sidelights in this matter. This cult has crept into our real life, imparting its values, values possibly never intended, but there all the same. For example, an honest question might be asked about a subconscious motivation in "Jockism"—a quest for the meaning of masculinity. Is the renewed accent on athletic prowess due in part to a revolt against longhaired peaceniks (young men), would-be intellectuals (young men), who are rejecting the "manly" ideal? Is it an attempt to put them down by reasserting that a real man is one who plays the game all the way?

Another gloomy feature to note is the amount expended by Catholic high schools and colleges on this department. Athletic coaches are in high demand; good coaches get good money. They need staff assistants, and personnel/athletic budgets continue to soar. It would be interesting to run a study of 20 representative Catholic high schools in this country to compare the athletic budget, let us say, with the money expended for teachers and materials in the department of religion—or even English. Such a study might give graphic examples of where our priorities are.

All man-made religions run their course. Perhaps in time, St. Jock may join the list of dis-

qualified saints. Right now, however, he reigns
with great strength. Each fall his image is vener-
ated on thousands of television screens as wor-
shippers (who grow fussy at a Mass that goes more
than 45 minutes) will pay dutiful attention to him
for a three or four hour sitting on a Sunday. Peace
to St. Jock. To him we pray for winning, playing the
game, and always, victory! Never failure, never
defeat, never surrender!

ANTI-HEROES

It took a book to open the eyes to our present lack
of heroes in public life, thus dramatizing our jock
heroes as plastic replacements. Joe McGinniss,
journalist-author, in 1968 wrote *The Selling of the
President,* an instant success. He told how TV used
Madison Avenue techniques and cosmetics to
make Richard Nixon a sellable product, a possible
president. McGinniss dropped out of sight for eight
years, then reappeared with his book, *Heroes.* He
has been silent since. McGinniss set out in late
1972 to discover why there were no longer any
American heroes. The report of that search
(*Heroes*) is interesting. When he intersperses
details of his journey looking for the lost American
hero with information about his own life, and his
own loss as hero when he left his wife and children
to take up a sometime relationship with another
woman, you get intimations of our real loss in
America.

McGinniss is (was) a Catholic; his wife was a Catholic. His personal journey appeared to be a search for a different lost hero: a father. McGinniss resembles those archetypal juveniles in Ross MacDonald's Lew Archer novels, one of those young people looking in the recalled past for some clue to his troubled present; both past and present are bitter. McGinniss' father meant to be an architect as his father was. He never made it and ended up only making blueprints for architects. Joe's maternal uncle was a monsignor, a "successful" Massachsetts Irish priest. The elder McGinniss, who from Joe's description would be a "loser," met his wife, 13 years his senior and the Irish Catholic daughter of a New York City fireman, on a sea voyage. Joe was born when his mother was 40, after two miscarriages. Their only child-son was reared carefully, closely, guardedly, lest he hurt himself and die before manhood. McGinniss speaks well, if ideally, about Catholic school training. It seems that his Catholic education filled him with desires for almost impossible goodness and sanctity, so that he could "please God, and please my mother."

Yet it was the lost father the author was really looking for. The father tried but could not express affection; he turned out to be an alcoholic. The elder McGinniss started a travel service which went broke, and in the end he just died of weariness. Such a marriage especially took its toll on the mother. She fell into the states of depression, also turned to drink and ended up with periods in a hospital for mental depression. She never really found the happiness that Joe wanted for her, or for his father.

You feel sorry for the wife and children Joe left; you are wounded for him and for the woman he dallies with. Most of all, you grieve for what happened before Joe was born: how the wrong people marry, how demands are made by the young on the old for things the old cannot deliver, and how demands are made by the old on the young for the things the young should not be forced to deliver.

Behind the McGinniss facade is alcohol. Every member of the hero set that Joe encounters becomes for him someone to test in a drinking bout. To him, they are all weak as he feels weak; they all seem to have the hidden fears he has. The search for Joe McGinniss' hero is a search for lost innocence, and a kind of father he needed but never had.

Heroes was different from stories by ex-Catholics in one way. McGinniss didn't blame Catholic education, nor put it down. There was no attack on nuns for falsehoods, hypocrisies, or failures as persons. That is not true of other books by ex-Catholics, who report such shortcomings as common in Catholic teachers of the 40s and 50s. Was that your experience? Our teachers (30s, early 40s), mostly nuns, were never Ph.D.s or M.A.s but they performed a fair job of education. Our Catholic schooling did not isolate

or inhibit us. We were able to move into the outside world if we wanted to, even if "Catholics
were different." So could it not be true that some
of those ex-Catholics who blame their falling
away from the Church on nuns and priests encountered in their grade school learning years,
are transferring blame? Are they not really trying
to alibi themselves in many ways? Yes, one or the
other of our teacher-nuns was strange. Many of
us share stories of one famous nun who wielded
her power a little strongly, or another who had
some eccentricities. But was that not true of
public school teachers too? Such attacks on our
past Catholic schooling from our present understanding of the Church is cowardly; it is based on
a time when we had no such understanding. We
had that viewpoint for that time; now we have a
different view.

To blame the past for what we know now is to
write revisionist history, which is unfair. All of us
have to accept ourselves at maturity. We can no
longer blame the past for our present selves. We
accept responsibility for what we are today.

The fate of Joe McGinniss might have been
turned by the fact that his father, who couldn't
make it as an architect, married an older woman
(and Freudians might say, a mother figure), and so
he turned to alcohol. His son, who had such great
expectations and ideals, never found those ideals
in his father or in himself. Young McGinniss also
turned to alcohol and searched in "love" for
solace: the story of so many modern American

men. Yet McGinniss and all of us have to take the responsibility for our own lives. We either have to accept what we are, or do something about it. We learn to live with us, to say yes to us, and if possible, to love us.

That may be the true hero needed in our day— the person who assumes responsibility for the present state of his life. His is like the "house built on the rock." He is not subject to whims and shifts of current, nor ultra-sensitive to unreasonable demands made on him by others to conform to their image. In that case there are modern heroes, but probably such heroes are few.

Winners, losers; in, out; up, down. We vacillate quickly—quicker than ever before. And it's all fashionable—if it sells, if it can be promoted, if it can make money, if it is chic.

CHIC

Tom Wolfe is not everybody's favorite writer. The journalist made his fame on the old *Herald Tribune,* and since then has free-lanced. Wolfe writes with exclamation points, strange adjectives in profusion, using all the "in" words to such an extent the writing becomes parody. His first book, *The Kandy-Kolored Tangerine-Flake Stream-Line Baby,* about the eccentricities of the Hollywood life-style, got him into the big time. Another book took on the New York art establishment for promoting ugliness as art. His last book, *Mauve Gloves*

and Madmen, Clutter and Vine, was another collection of essays about the American scene.

Wolfe loves to use the word "chic" when he
dissects new life-style patterns. He demolished
Leonard Bernstein and others when he described
their "Radical Chic," when these affluent New
York artists gave parties for Black Panthers in the
lovely, rich homes of the New York arty set.
Wolfe's latest variation is the phrase "funky
chic." "Funky" is a word that came out of the rock
and music idiom; it means blues, earthy. "Funky
chic" is used by Wolfe to describe the fashions
once used by the counterculture but readopted
and claimed by the Establishment. These would
be blue jeans, love beads, bandannas, Indian
blouses, painter's overalls and work shirts.
"Chic" is French in origin, but it may be a variation on "chicane" trickery, which in turn may
come from the Middle European word "tzigane,"
gypsy—i.e., a trickster. In a way, "chic" is
trickery, a kind of disguise.

As Wolfe puts it, anti-fashion became fashion,
as is clear from the designs (gypsy-like) from Paris
for feminine fashions in which fabrics are disguised as rags, but are purchased at a substantial
price. The author is right to point out that fashion
is tied in with politics and philosophy. Wolfe cites
the conventional idea that fashion is really a kind
of a front one chooses to place between the outer
world and his real self. But then Wolfe wants to
extend the idea. He describes new meanings for

fashion. The fashion makes the soul. The real self is the product of outside influences, including fashion, on a person's status.

That description works. One only has to look at what change of fashion has done even to things that were presumed to be settled, finished. An example may help here. Is the woman in the pants suit, using jewelry, hair finely coiffed, the same person who last year was bundled up in a religious habit? When this woman changed one kind of fashion (nun) for another (woman), was her personality affected? Did she become "liberated?" Did the convenience, color, adaptability of the fashions she could now buy open her up to life, new experience? Some would answer no, the woman basically is the same person she was. Others would say yes, and indicate that change is bad. The new kinds of fashion have opened her to certain ("wrong") kinds of experiences which a nun should not have. Others, and include us here, say yes, it would open her to new experiences, but no, the experiences are not necessarily bad, but yes, some could have been bad because she was not ready for them, but maybe it was good because it helped her to mature by emerging, as it were, from a cocoon to the air of life. Notice: the new clothing choices for nuns were not the styles of the poor, nor the rich. The choice is mostly middle class. Here the sister finds her identity as person. Although, so help us, blue denim habits have appeared.

The style of vestments does send off vibrations. Do you really want to receive Communion from a guy dressed in an ever-changing kind of cocoon, ornamented with a halo of purple and mauve which he calls a stole? Are we to believe that the triumphalism and power of the Church, which the old vestments symbolized (they say), are better replaced by the velours and satins and new brocades in pop colors? Young men rejected the cassock because it was too feminine (all those skirts) and then out-dressed Aimee Semple Mc-Pherson with flowing robes in oatmeal color. Now they have both: cassock (again) and the robes.

Note the ways the priest, particularly the religious priest, wishes to advertise himself as casual, open and responsible, with a T-shirt, a shirt with collars but without ties, or tie sloppily hung around the neck. Here the male is more funky chic. Few nuns' clothes have gone corduroy, leather, earth colors. But the male, ah, he's gone funky and has outdone the poor man in choice of raggy fabrics.

Consider even the funky chic of certain liturgical fabrics or ornaments. We have swung away from the Gothic and Baroque. We have achieved ecclesial plastic, gimcrackery ceramic and patina-ed tin. "Funky chic" is in the Church.

We find our new person and meaning for self and faith in the fashions that adopt us and send out messages we never dreamed of. We were told the old thing symbolized the old and outmoded

Church. Yet what does the new chic symbolize? That may be a terrible question to ask, still more to answer. Because the answer may simply tell us that for some, Church "person" is surface glitter, softness and smothering. That's an improvement?

Worse, have we Christians given in to display and embraced the pomps of the devil?

POMPS

A standard formula of the Catholic faith is the baptismal promise. These promises were made only once, at baptism. Now they are very much part of Confirmation. Each year, too, they are repeated by the congregation at the Vigil Mass on Holy Saturday, or at the Easter Sunday Mass. The Latin text began, "Do you renounce Satan," and then in the old translation of the Latin words, "and all his pomps?" In the present version used in America, for the word "pomps," "and all his empty promises" has been substituted. "Empty promises" is not a correct translation for "pomps," and is a comedown from "pomps." But then, it has never been exactly clear to the majority of Christians what these pomps of the devil were. We all renounced them but what we were renouncing was never certain. "The empty promises" of Satan may have some meaning, but even here, we wager, if you asked what was meant, you'd get a vacant stare.

Look up the word "pomps" in the *Dictionary of Word Origins*, and you will learn it derives from the Latin and Greek. "Pompa" had something to do with a procession, an especially sumptuous one. Another reading says it was "organized magnificence." A Latin dictionary describes it to mean some kind of a grandiose banquet. These banquets must have influenced the Church Fathers so much for the worse that they were repelled by the word. So Christians were to renounce "banquets of the devil." From this came the French word "pomper," to dress oneself magnificently. Then along came words like "pompon," ornamental decorations but useless, or even the word "pumps" for slippers, not really meant for walking. All our negative words, "pompous," "pomposity," originate in the same word—someone not real, somebody or something inflated. Yet, in short, it would appear that the early Fathers were unhappy with display, munificence. For a while, English substituted another phrase: we were asked to renounce Satan and all his "displays."

Canon 138 says that clerics are to stay away from those kinds of deeds and works which men think are unbecoming to the clerical state, specifically those which are in conflict with their calling. Among these are games of chance. They are not to habitually indulge in gambling for money. (How about clerics at Las Vegas?) They should not frequent bars, saloons. Canon 140 says they should not be present at shows, dances and "pomps" which are not fitting for them. The canon uses "pompa" and a commentary says it means "a parade or any form of public pageantry either in connection with worship or with occasions of a very different sort" (Bouscaren). Yet, once more, we really do not know what pomps are. Big bashes? Mardi Gras festivals?

It would appear that while Christians renounce these pomps, culturally we are caught up in them. Clerics wear shoes with pompons, useless buckles and ornaments, or boots with gaudy decorations. Clerics and religious wear clothes which are frivolous, highly ornamented, and which, if the Fathers of the Church saw them, would cause these hallowed men to throw up their hands. Clerics and religious automatically put on the displays of the world. Even some episcopal dress, ceremonials and liturgies seem to reek more of "pompa," display than of liturgy. You see we are all caught up in this dichotomy between displays for the Lord and display for the sake of display; if not displays of the devil.

But there is one form of "pompa" in vogue which causes dismay here. How many Catholics are there now who are wearing that gold, silver, or ivory "cornuto," a horn-shaped ornament worn around the neck? The "cornuto," a horn, derives from the goat's horn. The goat is classically associated with the devil, sexual license and evil spirits (the god Pan, satyrs and orgies). According to Italian (and other) superstition, the wearing of the cornuto wards off the bad effects of the "evil eye," the "malocchio," which someone may want to put on you. Devil working against devil, as it were.

The amazing thing is that this superstitious emblem is being worn by Catholic men and women, young and old. It is rather startling at Confirmation and baptism to see people prominently wearing these horns. These good souls are at the same time renouncing the works and empty promises (pomps) of Satan. It is more difficult to trace the Sign of the Cross right above places where the "cornuto" is worn. The use of this has gone so far that priests are approached by devout Catholic persons (even nuns!) to bless these objects. (Priests are taught that in a pinch you could use the blessing for all things, but how can you bless a visible sign of the empty promises of the devil?) In defense it must be said that the people who wear these displays haven't the faintest idea what they are. It's the "in" decoration and it's an ornament. But if St. Chrysostom or St. Basil were to come back and see all the many Catholics wearing this devilish ornament, they would declare the devil had taken over.

The point is this: again we do not understand what we really do. Mindlessly, Catholics fall into the customs of the culture. Worse, we make little or no connection between what we say in the religious rite and how we act in a secular setting. We're all caught up in it—bishops, clerics, religious, laity. Indeed the works and empty promises of Satan are dangerous precisely because they appear so harmless and so right. Catho-

lics often not only do not practice what they
preach, they are not even aware of what is meant
when it is preached. We just don't know what we
mean when we say, "I believe."

But there are scores of others who want to tell
us what we should mean when we say "I believe."
Even worse, they want to change our belief to what
they want it to mean. They, a small elite, know better than the simple little Catholic.

Possibly the worst fault is our predilection in
America to speak down to the "ordinary" guy (that
makes us out of the ordinary). We have to advertise we know better than the rest. Everyone should
line up to follow the leader. A *New Yorker* cartoon
(April 28, 1975, page 48) shows two leprechauns
with pointed hats chatting under a convenient
toadstool. One is saying to the other, "Who do you
think will really do the most for the little people—
George Wallace, Fred Harris, Jimmy Carter, Scoop
Jackson, or Mo Udall?" In one sharp stroke, the
author of the cartoon, D. Reilly, captured that
ridiculous catchphrase, which appears in politics,
in education, and in the Church. "The little
people" is a tendency to speak down to the
average man, to assign him the status of minor,
someone who needs a loving, kind and powerful
father to watch over him lest he be led down
garden paths, be swindled of his goods, or
betrayed by crafty and conniving people. Notice
how many politicians speak loftily of their dedica-
tion to protect the little man. See how editors
agitate against a law because "it will hurt the

simple people." Hear the cautions to beware of this or that opponent because he cares only for the rich and powerful and not for the little people.

This happens as much in the universities. There professors teach students that no matter what things they may have learned at home, in the homes of little people, simple people, average people, now they will receive new kinds of knowledge which will place them light years above their parents. The invitation is clear: they will become, in a sense, the intellectual custodians of their parents and ancestors.

The one place this tendency appears most markedly, of course, is in religion, where leaders, opinion-makers and activists have a dim view of the status of the average Catholic. Such are the elite Catholics who know the inside issues, who have studied at the feet of great sociologists, psychologists, and doctors of the law, but whose task it now is to protect the little man. Better still, it is their duty, as they see it, to uplift him, to bring him to the fuller light of understanding of what the faith asks of him in this day, according to their (the elite) version of the Good News.

(Our view is in no way to be conceived as an anti-intellectual stance. The true intellectual never talks down to people or pities their simplicity. The real intellectual knows that his role is not to gaze down on his brothers in the human flesh from some high peak and take pity on them by condescending to give them his view and his knowledge. Rather he considers himself one

241

with them in the human condition; he shares learning that he may learn from their native intelligence, that wisdom of experience and life which only time and maturity can confer.)

These would-be saviors and new messiahs feel that they and only they now understand what kind of demands are made on a Catholic in the latter part of the 20th century. Zealous missionaries for themselves, they seek to change opinions by forcing the average man, the little man to face up to their interpretations of faith. Some delight to make Mr. Simple Man understand that the troubles of today are his fault, because he is not truly living the faith in this social age. They would become self-appointed guardians of the simple people by "raising their consciousness."

Consider that great intellectual, Cardinal John Henry Newman. Every seminary, every gathering of priests and nuns involved in retreat work, conference work, study work, seminar work, CCD work, should read Newman *On Consulting the Faithful on Matters of Doctrine* as standard background. They could learn from this most civil saint that there exists among the faithful the consensus of a faith, far deeper and truer than any sociological study. Cardinal Newman held that it is essential for leaders of the Church to keep in touch with the "faithful" (who are not that "simple"). The reflected faith of the faithful is ever a good sounding board for any explorations into the perennial faith of the people of God.

The point is that such elite, but separated

leaders and makers of opinion, insult the flock. The "little" people are not little. They have survived in a faithless world by the God-given gift of common sense. We must understand that people (the "prudent men" of Aquinas fame) have a built-in detector of what is genuine and true, versus what is spurious and false. Leaders must not indulge in condescension. A fruitful meditation on Ephesians brings the reminder that the Lord Jesus took upon Himself the form of a servant to become one like us. *One like us.* He assumed our common humanity; became a "little man." He shared our bread, our life, our culture. Never did He reject the wisdom of faith that He found as He did in the Syro-Phoenician woman, in the Roman centurion, in the woman who poured ointment over His feet, in Simon Peter who recognized Him as a special Person. Bury once and for all the concept of the "little fellow." We could discover, especially in matters of faith, that the little fellow is more of a giant than we ever could be.

L'ENVOI

Have you ever wondered when reading poems of old, as you came to that last stanza and met the phrase, "l'envoi," what that meant? Literally, "a sending on the way," or another way to put it would be "one for the road." (It reminds you of Kerouac's *On the Road,* or maybe the movie, *Two for the Road.*) In literary terms the "envoy" was the final stanza used in the ballade (or ballad). The ballade, which is a special verse form, has the last line of the first stanza appearing as the refrain in each of the stanzas. Thus, "l'envoi" sent us on our way, echoing the refrain of each stanza. As we get ready to depart, what has been the "envoy," the refrain of this book?

Anyone who has persevered to this point should have guessed by now what hopes are herein held for sanity, humor, reason, awareness, patience. Add two more ingredients.

The theme of reconciliation, invoked but never used for the late Holy Year, is one that is most pertinent in our day. Very few would deny it is one we all desperately need. But even if reconciliation is something so desired, where do you begin? To help the dialogue, let's bring back an idea proposed ten years ago, but never publicized.

The suggestion comes from the late Anglican poet, Wystan Hugh Auden, whose words, both in poetry and prose, continue to live. In his introduction to a 1964 book, *The Protestant Mystics* edited by Anne Fremantle, Auden proposed that possibly we might all just have misread the meaning of Pentecost as related in Chapter 2 of the Acts of the Apostles. As the author put it, "The miracle wrought by the Holy Spirit is generally referred to as the gift of tongues; is it not equally the gift of ears?" Auden sees the miracle of that day in the fact not that strangers in Jerusalem could speak in different tongues. What was more marvelous was that strangers as well as Galileans could understand one another, despite the language barrier.

We thought the Tower of Babel was a curse because it produced a multiplicity of human languages. Yet Auden comments, that was not the curse. Diversity is a rich and necessary gift to human life. The evil of that incident was rather that each one at that abominated place was convinced that his own language was the proper and only mode of communication. Those who spoke differently were evidently lesser, more prone to error, and probably dishonest. Babel proposed that truth was reserved not only to one's own language, but even to one's own personal interpretation of that language. (In fact, Peter Farb's book, *Word Play,* makes you wonder how we humans can communicate at all.) Auden reminds us that on Pentecost Day, before the people of Jerusalem could speak, first they had to listen to the strange tongues of others and then translate that into their own meaning.

This is not meant to be a discussion of the implications of Pentecostalism. Still it is curious that in our time when we are engulfed and swamped by words on every side, Pentecostalism states that certain individuals believe the Holy Spirit is speaking in a special way through them. Within the Pentecostal phenomenon there are also people who claim to understand what is said by others speaking "with the gift of tongues." But on a numerical basis alone, more claim to speak with God's accents than those who claim to understand. Pentecostals do not, it is true, claim that God is speaking uniquely through them. The implication comes through that some Pentecostals might think that it is by their speech that God adds to the storehouse of religious experience.

Back to what Auden precisely proposes: should we not begin to speak of the "gift of ears" as a truly Christian experience? Jesus said frequently, "He who has ears to hear, let him hear." If we are to follow Him, hearing is a paramount need. The gift of ears is not a judgment about moderns and the noisy clamor which provides the background to today's culture. The idea behind this gift is to remind us that instead of proclaiming what we want or what we think, is it not time for us to take some time for pause, and listen to what others are actually saying? In the developing science of semiotics (words as signs), philosophers point out that the person who uses the word as a sign intends one idea, and the person who interprets the word, the sign, may receive an entirely different concept. Our need is to reduce all those factors which lead to breakdown between the person who uses words and the person who hears them. So "to hear" means in a sense being willing to enter the other person's sphere. The "gift of ears," in another variation of the scriptural idea, asks us to deny ourselves, to die to ourselves, to put one kind of seed into the ground that it may emerge with a new way of life.

To allow the "gift of ears" to bring this about is penance. This is hardship. It is an art not easily achieved. It presupposes that we begin by accepting as a given fact that the other speaks in truth.

We cannot abitrarily assign malice, bad judgment and misinformation to others. This kind of hearing asks us to be willing to consider the possibility that our position can always be open to reconsideration. To put it more positively, this hearing process allows us to show how we are open to growth, to learn more about others, to understand their whys and wherefores, to consider that the reasons others disagree with us may be genuine.

The attempt to use this "gift of ears" is always penitential. If we could all grow quiet, stop proclaiming so much what I see, what I believe, what I want, what I need, in order to listen to others, truly listen, to hear as if others were speaking for the first time. What a great gift, what a chance for understanding, what a possiblility for growth! The curse of Babel was that in his pride, each person there thought that only he spoke in God's accents. The gift of ears turns this idea around. It makes us believe that it is possible, just possible, that others too may be speaking in God's accents—yes, even to us.

And possibly, to still this maddening pace that kills young men, or gets us all into a need for therapy, or the desire to cop out of it all, can we propose sauntering into the next century? Again, the idea comes from the Benedictine Dom Debuyst.

SAUNTERING

In the 18th and 19th centuries there was a movement to interpret words and their derivation in a romantic way. "Romantic," that is to say, not in the meaning of love but in the meaning of idealistic and extravagant interpretation.

Henry David Thoreau, much in vogue these days, once wrote on "Walking" (*Atlantic Monthly*, June 1862). He expressed the concept that the word "sauntering" derived from a period during the Middle Ages when "idle people rode about the country and asked charity under the pretense of going 'a la Sainte Terre,' that is, to the Holy Land." So the children would point him out as "a Sainte-Terrer, a Holy Lander."

Later writers tried to explain origins of this word from "sans terre"—someone who had no land, someone who had no home.

Modern etymology disdains such romantic explanations. The latest dictionary proposes that the word comes from the Middle English word "to muse or to brood," thus, someone walking around leisurely, not knowing what to do or where to go, and wrapped in contemplation. Still another description says that the word comes from "s'avancer"—to advance oneself, to move forward, but something to do with the way of walking—that is, instead of going in a direct manner, one goes off to the side, obliquely, of course we would say today.

Whatever the explanation, Thoreau's interpretation captured an ever-present spirit in American literature. As he put it, "The man who saunters is not a vagrant, but someone who is at home anywhere, or is at home in the world." As the New

England writer said, the saunterer "is no more vagrant than the meandering river which is all the while sedulously seeking the shortest course to the sea."

It is interesting to note how many saunterers there still are today, the young street people of America drifting along the highways with no fixed goal. Even feminine fashions have caught this mood and spirit of sauntering—the gypsy-like clothes, the styles which belong to no one period and which are for every period.

Now it is all walking, jogging, and the latest, running. Yet sauntering is a facet of our tradition, but Americans are suspicious of sauntering. We have been brought up to believe that a man should know where he's going, should have his course and direction clearly mapped out as soon as possible. Every time one reads the Gospel according to St. Luke and hears that Jesus had fixed his course steadfastly on Jerusalem, the message is clear. The Western Christian ethic holds that like the Lord we should have our face set directly towards our goal, and never be turned aside from its pursuit. The fact that Jesus detoured and went off through this town and that town, we forget. To saunter is frivolous, and thus not Christian.

Perhaps Thoreau was right. Everyone has his own Holy Land, towards which he more or less is heading, or to which he wants to go. The terrain of that Holy Land may not be known to the saunterer. Indeed it can be wrongly apprehended, until a clearer vision intervenes. It may be when we arrive at what we thought was our desired Holy Land, it turns out not to be what we wanted at all. So we begin to saunter once more.

Not all will accept this view that sauntering may not be bad at all, and in fact may be a good thing. We are not speaking of idle drifting or aimless wandering. (But then, why not?) We are proposing that too much of modern life demands a pace and tempo that kills the spirit. To be able to wander through familiar landscapes of the soul in search of the unfamiliar in these stereotyped days can be most refreshing. Not to be tied down to a specific period in life, when one must assume a specific task or obligation allows the spirit to be freer in seeking out its own Holy Land. To saunter is not to be a vagabond (which is a "bad" word; a vagabond, even in scripture, is not a good thing to be) in the negative sense. To saunter means that one must take time to observe the landscape, to espouse the unusual, to see the familiar with new eyes, and so be prepared to find one's Holy Land in the most unexpected of places.

So thank you for sauntering throught this book. Thank you for listening to one person's reflections. It would be nice if our meeting had been a dialogue. Possibly it has been. Throughout these pages the author has tried to saunter through the landscape of the day to point out this and to note that, in the hope that these are things others may have noticed and wondered about. But better still it is to be hoped that others will point out to him what he has missed.